Blitzkrieg

The Art of War in the Spirit

Tony George

Tony George Ministries/The
Remnant of Jacob
Chicago, Illinois

Tony George

Blitzkrieg: The Art of War in the Spirit

Unless otherwise indicated, all scriptural quotations are from the King James Version of the Bible.

Comments from Sun Tzu's The Art of War

Cover photo by Carlos Gutierrez/UPI press Latin America

To Contact Evangelist Tony George for appointments, seminars, Mass Deliverances, and engagements please email me @

tonygeorgeministries@gmail.com
myspace.com/tonygeorgeministries
facebook.com/remnantofjacob

To order a copy of Blitzkrieg and other Books go to Amazon.com or to the Createspace.com/3374692

Also available is "Getting into Position": The Remnant of Jacob go to Amazon.com or Createspace.com/3389564

Blitzkrieg: The Art of War in the Spirit

Table of Contents

Forward

And from the days of John the Baptist until now, the kingdom of Heaven suffereth violence, and the violent take it by force.
Matthew 11:12

Mountain of fire prayer , destroying satanic covenants
PRAYERS: -

1) Jesus the Man of War, arise, scatter every satanic rage against me and my family in the name
of Jesus
2) Altars of satanic transaction raised against me in the heavens, on earth or in the waters, Holy
Ghost destroy them by thunder, by fire in the name of Jesus.
3) Powers of enchantment and divination working against my life die in the name of Jesus.

SONG: - Deliver me, deliver me, deliver oh Lord, by Your power by Your fire, deliver me oh Lord.

Galatians 3:13 Christ hath redeemed us from the curse of the law, being made a curse for us: for it is

written, Cursed *is* every one that hangeth on a tree:
Galatians 3:14 That the blessing of Abraham might come on the Gentiles through Jesus Christ; that we might receive the promise of the Spirit through faith.

4) Polygamous curse troubling my life break and die in the name of Jesus
5) Consequences of polygamous curses in my life Blood of Jesus reverse them in the name of
Jesus.
6) Evil umbrella covering my glory be roasted in the name of Jesus.

Dedications

I also dedicate this book to the Legacy of Win Worley and his books on warfare prayers (#4) and the ministry of deliverance that is still going strong at Hegewisch Baptist Church. Hbcdelivers.org

I also want to acknowledge the prayers, leadership, inspiration, and the laying on of hands of these true Pentecostal soldiers of Zion:

Apostle R.D. Henton, a man that God has and still is using mightily and my inspiration for ministry and without fear to walk in the vocation in which I am called, I truly thank God for my Shepherd and a true Apostolic Father in the Gospel;

Mother Kathryn Bynum for those hugs, prayers and holiness teachings; **Mother Bernice Davis** for her example of dedication to the deliverance ministry; **Mother Hopkins** for her counsel, encouragement and sincere heart; **Pastor Mike Therior@ HBC**

Mother Mae Dupree for a walk with God that made me more hungry for God; **Mother Sykes** for praying when God told her to;

Pastor Chris Desilva and **Min. Kemi**; and **Dr. D.K. Olukoya** and all **the Mountain of Fire Miracle ministry family in Chicago** and worldwide for the first-hand teaching and training in hand-to-hand combat against spiritual wickedness;

Evangelist Alice "Kindness" Bonk for her wisdom and the Ministry of Deliverance, what a blessing she has been in my life; and

Evangelist Jennifer Busa for her gift and revelation for prophetic prayers!! I thank God for these vessels of honor whose hands are clean and whose hearts are pure, that can stand in the presence of

God and get a prayer through. God bless the Tuesday prayer and the Prayer Warriors Ministry.

I want to give special thanks for the life, wisdom, and mentorship of **(the Prophet) Dr. Thomas "Dad" Bynum, Jr**.

 I truly miss you!!! I thank God for these ministry gifts and all the intercessors that God has quickened to bombard heaven throughout the world to pray me through!!!! Shalom

I want give special thanks, blessings, and acknowledgment to Apostle John Eckhardt for his the book "Prays that routs Demons" and to Dr. N. Cindy Trimm for her book "The Rules of Engagement".

These books were an inspiration for me to develop and to write this book.

This book of warfare prayers of annihilation is nothing more than the fruit that of these 2 titles, that this Great Man and Woman of God bared.

"By your fruit you shall know them" I want them to both know personally that they are bearing great fruit which is much needed in these endtimes to the ministry of Spiritual Warfare.

Shalom again!!

Introduction

<u>Blitzkrieg The Lightning War</u>

Blitzkrieg was based on speed, co-ordination, and movement. It was designed to hit hard and move on instantly. Its aim was to create panic amongst the civilian **(and in this case the demonic)** population.

A civilian population on the move can be absolute havoc for a defending army trying to get its forces to the war front. Doubt, confusion, and rumor were sure to paralyze both the government and the defending military.

"Speed, and still more speed, and always speed was the secret ... and that demanded audacity, more audacity, and always audacity."

They all postulated that tanks could not only seize ground by brute strength, but could also be the central factor in a new strategy of warfare.

If moved rapidly enough, concentrations of tanks could smash through enemy lines and into the enemy's rear, destroying supplies and artillery positions and decreasing the enemy's will to resist.

All of them found tanks to be an ultimate weapon able to penetrate deep into enemy territory while followed by infantry and supported by artillery and air force.

German High Command used Spanish Civil War (1936-38) as a testing ground for newly developed tactics, which proved to be a formidable combination of land and air action.

This combined use of mobile units and air power was possible by the extensive use of radio and communication network. It was soon known as Blitzkrieg - Lightning War.

From October of 1940 to March of 1941, Germans conquered Balkans using the same proven tactics. When in June of 1941, Germany invaded Russia, tactics of Blitzkrieg allowed them to reach the outskirts of Moscow in December of 1941.

Tactics of Blitzkrieg were also implemented with great success by Erwin Rommel in North Africa (1941-1943). Since late 1942, the outnumbered German Army was fighting a defensive war on two fronts and was unable to launch any major offensives with exception of Kursk (June of 1943) and Ardennes (December of 1944) offensive.

Overall, tactics of Blitzkrieg were the main contributor of early German victories (1939-1942), when German supply base and logistics were able to maintain the speed of the advancing units.

At the same time, the potential of Blitzkrieg and related tactics were fully appreciated by the Allies, who implemented its tactics on all fronts. U.S. Army General George Patton used Blitzkrieg and mobile warfare tactics in his European operations of 1944.

 After World War II, tactics of Blitzkrieg and mobile warfare developed by the Germans were used by Israel in the Yom Kippur War, as well as by American forces during the Operation Desert Storm.

Overall, tactics of Blitzkrieg are based on coordinated, concentrated and precise air and land attacks to provide a rapid and powerful punch through the enemy lines in order to eventually encircle the enemy and/or to capture there strategic position.

Important factor behind mobile warfare was communication between the HQ and field units and vice-versa, as well as prepared starting points along with supply base and logistics to maintain the speed of the initial attack.

Although, it is often forgotten that surprise was also very important to the success of Blitzkrieg and that is why Germany never declared war on any country that it attacked. The revolutionary tactics of Blitzkrieg and mobile warfare developed during World War II formed a base for future development of weaponry and warfare.

The Concept of Blitzkrieg

Airforce attacks enemy front-line and rear positions, main roads, airfields and communication centers. At the same time infantry attacks on the entire frontline (or at least at main places) and engages the enemy. This restrains the enemy from knowing where the main force will attack and makes it impossible to prepare any defenses.

Concentrated tank units break through main lines of defense and advance deeper into enemy territory, while following mechanized units pursuit and engage defenders preventing them from establishing defensive positions. Infantry continues to engage enemy to misinform and keep enemy forces from withdrawing and establishing effective defense.

Infantry and other support units attack enemy flanks in order to link up with other groups to complete the attack and eventually encircle the enemy and/or capture strategic position.

Mechanized groups spearhead deeper into the enemy territory, outflanking the enemy positions, and paralyzing the rear, preventing withdrawing troops and defenders from establishing effective defensive positions. Main forces link up encircling and cutting off the enemy.

Biblical Blitzkrieg

This was the World War II version of warfare implemented by mankind. But if you study the bible in the conquest of Canaan, God had HIS own version of Blitzkrieg. In the Book of Joshua in the first 13 chapters all you see is Blitzkrieg the way it was done in the time the bible was written, except that the aerial attack came from the Host of Heaven.

In Chapter 12 you see the recount of the conquering of the 31 kings which today is significant of the giants we must conquer in the spirit.

I highly suggest that you also read the first 8 chapters of the book of Judges so you will get an idea of Biblical Blitzkriegs. Read how Gideon and his 300 men slew 120,000 Midianites and their hired mercenaries. Read how the host of heaven went to battle with Barack and Deborah.

One thing to remember is that the ancient Israelites in the ancient Blitzkriegs didn't have tanks, airplanes, and ships. No, these battles were fueled and facilitated by God himself and his greatest weapons were those with faith and courage, who were out-numbered, but yet that HE anointed them mightily for the task and wrought victory after victory.

The giants that they contended with back then are like the spiritual giants that we have to contend with today, like the spirit of Jezebel who operates her witchcraft and whoredoms in the local and mega churches. **This spirit is the principality behind all charismatic witchcraft.** This spirit also defies leadership and the 5-fold ministry gifts, and is also preaching and using her prophetic gift and mind control in the pews and the pulpit.

The spirit of Absalom who develops its own form of leadership, groups, clicks, all that goes against the vision of the ministry that God has given the Leader, a spirit that will also challenge the anointing and the vision that God has given that Leader. I pray that he gets caught and hung in a tree in Jesus' name.

The Spirit or the anointing of Balaam and all those who prostitute the gift of God for money, and all those that are hired to curse the innocent through witchcraft; oh we cannot also forget those that are preaching the doctrine of Balaam.

Lilith the screech owl and her team of spirit spouses that form the unit of marriage-breaking spirits, spirits of rape and destitution, and these along with Serium the Satyr, the spirit of Ghetto.

The Black widows who lure people into their web of control and manipulation. These are just to name a few of the powers and principalities in operation along with the spirit of the anti-Christ connected with the spirit of homosexuality that has infiltrated not only the pews and the choir stand, but the pulpit.

This book of prayers is designed to release the raw power of the Kingdom of God, to rage war on the kingdom of darkness. God told Jeremiah to root out, pull down, to destroy, and to overthrow, and then you build and plant. (Jer 1:10).

We have gotten this thing backwards. That's why we are not walking in the power of the early church. There is too much compromise, control, and manipulation using the word of God to build the kingdom of man instead of just plain old gospel preaching, praying, laying hands on the sick and casting out devils which is the foundation of The Kingdom of God.

People are crying out to God for help, a help that can only be attained through prayer and fasting and the word of God. It is imperative that we get educated in the spirit and in the supernatural and no longer be deceived by the enemy's devices. Those of you that are battling witchcraft, the bible has a remedy, not the herbalist; everything you need is in the word of God.

I do not suggest that you go to any occult web sites to get information or to get any books on witchcraft to fight against it. There is a spirit that comes behind that, that will oppress you, and overtake you and you will wind up operating in it. You will wind up being messed up in church, speaking in tongues and operating in both worlds, and under a Jezebelic anointing. I don't care who you are, the risk is high going this route for no one knows the depths of satan. You've been warned and your blood is off my head.

I also do not advocate fighting witchcraft with witchcraft. No, this book of prayers is not about that. In the scriptures, the word of God deals with returning the witchcraft that was sent at you back to the senders source and destroying the demonical powers of those works that is infecting and affecting your lives. The other is God's wrath and judgment against the works, not the people. **Now if the person or persons don't stop and repent from what they are doing, well that's between them and God.** In every case or situation, God has the final decision for HE is the Righteous Judge.

I also do not advocate calling out people's names that are working iniquity. In all the Psalms, not one time did David call out a person's name; he just referred to them as his enemies which in turn became the enemies of God HIMSELF. The reason for this is that you start forming anger or resentment against that person or persons and then even though they are wrong your prayers become sin, and are not heard by God. Now through resentment, anger, and hatred you have crossed the line and no longer stand in the righteousness of God, but in the wickedness of satan.

I suggest you read Rev. 2:20-24, because this was the testimony of Jesus Christ of how we have allowed these spirits to influence his servants.

I have seen this too many times. Even if you use to operate in witchcraft and you've gotten saved and filled with the Holy Ghost, you still need to renounce it, all oaths and covenants. Ask God to break all the dedications, curses and spells you have made. Get it purged out of your blood line and get those devils cast out of you. There is no short cut to this. I don't care who you think you are this is a must.

I suggest that you read the testimony of Pastor Irene Parks (The Witch that Switched). I highly suggest those of you that have made this mistake, burn, delete and destroy this material and go get some deliverance and get those spirits cast out of you.

There is plenty of Christian material written by Win Worley, Derrick Prince, Jessie Penn- Lewis, Frank Hammond, Dr. Angie Ray, Mother Ruth Brown, Dr. D.K. Olukoya, Apostle Ivory Hopkins, Apostle John Eckhardt, Apostle Kim Daniels, Bishop George Bloomer, Pastor Larry Huch, Bill Banks, Dr. A.O. Itiola, Dr. Cindy Trimm, Pastor Jonas Clark, Gene B. Moody, and others just to name a few that are dedicated to the ministry of deliverance and spiritual warfare that have written extensive material in exposing and doing spiritual warfare against witchcraft and demonic oppression. I also suggest highly demonbusters.com.

Note: There are many ministries and authors out there that deserve acknowledgement that I don't even know about. Even though I mentioned a few, don't feel like you were slighted. It is my prayer that your gift will make room for you and bring you before great men. We are in a day where we have to encourage and pray for one another, because we are at the top of the list when it comes to attacks from the enemy.

This book of prayers is just another one of the instruments of the Kingdom of God that God has released into the earth realm to wage war, bring victory and destroys the works of the devil. I highly suggest that if you have struggles in your life, like anger, resentment, lust, fornication, pride, or unforgiveness I suggest that you repent, forsake, and work on getting some deliverance before you enter into warfare on this level.

The Prayers in this book are conditional, conditional on the type of life you are living. There are those of us that are sincere that have struggles, and there are those that are fighting addictions and satanic forces. I suggest that repentance, forsaking sin, and praying for deliverance to receive deliverance. Deliverance is the key to be able to pray on this level. I don't want to exclude anybody for praying the prayers from this book, but deliverance is essential.

I pray that any prayer in this book that is prayed by a person who has sent witchcraft (even charismatic witchcraft) at a person, and the person that they sent it to returned it back to the sender and then can't handle the taste of their own medicine, and so, instead of repenting and getting delivered from the spirit of pride they go out and recruit people to help pray against that person!! Now that's what Jezebel did to Naboth in 1King 20 with the sons of Belial; and I pray that any person that will use any prayer or verse against any person from this book, I pray that it backfires on you and blows up in your face in the name of Jesus Christ of Nazareth.

It's a shame because I have seen people fall all because they were recruited in a battle without praying, discerning, or seeking God first to see if the person who recruited them is in the wrong or what type of spirit they operate under. In fact, any person that would recruit another person to pray against someone else is nothing more than a witch or warlock themselves. It does not matter if you are holy and have a position in the church, you are still a worker of iniquity and filthy in the eyesight of God.

Prov. 20:22: Say not thou, I will recompense evil; but wait on the LORD, and he shall save thee.

I've seen too many people praying against witchcraft and they are either knowingly operating in it, or they have a multiple personality disorder or schizophrenia in which they can effectively operate in both worlds. Trust me, I found out the hard way in the early stages of the deliverance ministry, that everybody isn't who they say they are. For there are ministers of satan that transform themselves into ministers of righteousness and if you open your spiritual eyes, you'll see it all the time.

Ezek. 18:21-24: But if the wicked will turn from all his sins that he hath committed, and keep all my statutes, and do that which is lawful and right, he shall surely live, he shall not die. All his transgressions that he hath committed, they shall not be mentioned unto him: in his righteousness that he hath done he shall live. Have I any pleasure at all that the wicked should die? sayeth the Lord GOD: and not that he should return from his ways, and live?

But when the righteous turneth away from his righteousness, and committeth iniquity, and doeth according to all the abominations that the wicked man doeth, shall he live? All his righteousness that he hath done shall not be mentioned: in his trespass that he hath trespassed, and in his sin that he hath sinned, in them shall he die.

Don't Lose Hope

Personally there is a great reward in warfare, because you find out who you are in God, and where you stand in the Kingdom of God. Put it this way, if the devil isn't fighting you, whether in your personal life or your ministry, then really you are no threat to his kingdom. In fact you can consider yourself to be part of his team waiting to receive instructions from a (ventriloquist) familiar spirit, which you think is the Holy Spirit.

But for those of you that are under oppression on every side and you got people praying against you, talking about you, telling lies on you and they don't even know you, consider yourself a threat to satan's kingdom; and on that note I welcome you to the club and above all else the hand of God is in your life.

There are those that are true prayer warriors that know the importance of deliverance and as you go through in the work of God, we often either go get a tune up (deliverance) not because of sin either, or God will simply purge us as we go up in the spirit through prayer and fasting. The cleansing process is necessary for the anointing of the Holy Ghost to fill you in depth.

Psalm 65:2-4 (KJV): O thou that hearest prayer, unto thee shall all flesh come. Iniquities prevail against me: as for our transgressions, thou shalt purge them away. Blessed is the man whom thou chooseth, and causeth to approach unto thee, that he may dwell in thy courts: we shall be satisfied with the goodness of thy house, even of thy holy temple.

Psalm 79:9 (KJV): Help us, O God of our salvation, for the glory of thy name: and deliver us, and purge away our sins, for thy name's sake.

The most successful candidate's in spiritual warfare are!!!

1. Those that have a conviction and know how to forgive people quickly no matter what the circumstance. I cannot stress this even more the importance of not allowing a root of bitterness or unforgiveness to take form in your heart cause you will miss God in the process.

2. Those that don't compromise and have a flat footed stand for being sanctified and living Holy before the Lord.

3. Those that don't flirt with charismatic witchcraft or with those that secretly operates in it.

4. And those that are dedicated and consecrated before the Lord to not only be filled with the HolySpirit but his Love.

These are the ones that God hears; these are the ones that can get a prayer through.

Those of you that have died and walking in Romans 6 will definitely be triumphant and will walk in the anointing of Invincibility, as did Joshua, Caleb, Gideon, Samson, Paul, Stephen, Phillip, David, Othanial, David's 3 mighty men, Deborah, Anna the Prophetess, and many others, that were heroes of faith that didn't care and were totally sold out.

Sold out? What do you mean by that? Sold out to the point that well here's my testimony. I decided years ago back in 1994, I told God when I was not saved, and on drugs that when I die, don't let me die like a dog!!! When I die, let me die for you, let me die doing something to help build your Kingdom.

It's as simple as that!! Why? Well we're going to die anyway; it may as well be for HIS Majesty's service!!! The only thing is that I want to be in the will of God and fulfill the will of God. Trust me in the final analysis it's worth it.

And when you sell out, the fear is gone. Then the anointing comes, but only when you sell out for HIS service. It is my prayer that you are deemed worthy to receive it and that the hand of God and HIS anointing will rest on your life.

When you go to war on this level in the heavens you feel the grace and the continual leading of the Holy Spirit. Some of you don't have a choice but to go to war violently in the spirit.

Important Instructions

The effectiveness of these prayers will depend on the type of life you live before God according to His word, not religion or organizational traditions; God is no respecter of persons. God doesn't care too much about your titles or what position you hold in the Church.

Psalm 24:3-6 (KJV): Who shall ascend into the hill of the LORD? or who shall stand in his holy place? He that hath clean hands, and a pure heart; who hath not lifted up his soul unto vanity, nor sworn deceitfully. He shall receive the blessing from the LORD, and righteousness from the God of his salvation. This is the generation of them that seek him that seek thy face, O Jacob.

Number 1. I am not an advocate of wishing or praying for people to get hurt or to die. That is not the intent of my heart or the purpose of this book. If a person is wishing or chanting death over another person's life and if it is returned unto them (the spirit in operation) and if the intents of their heart manifest in their life, then that's between them and God. If that same person that is speaking death against another person and God delivers the sender and if they get saved and go on living a clean life before God, that's between them and God. The important thing is to not get caught up in having anger or resentments!! Forgive them and move on!!!!

The key component is for God to remove and destroy the works of witchcraft that has been sent to target you, and that the people that the devil has access in using are bombarded so much that they repent from their works, get saved, and surrender to Christ.

Number 2. Have a heart of forgiveness. In fact before you go into battle, forgive those persons and learn to love them for they have no idea how weak they are to allow satan to use them. One of my biggest challenges was to forgive the people whom God showed me that were attacking me. I found out the whole purpose of having that fore-knowledge was to forgive first, then ask God to destroy those works. I found out in doing that the prayers are heard and answered. Yes, it does sound strange but Jesus himself forgave on the cross and spent 3 days and 3 nights going to war. He set free those that were captive, took the keys of hell and of death and when HE arose, he declared all power belongeth unto me in heaven and in earth.

Some of the greatest prayer warriors don't have a position in a church, nor do they need one, nor do they get caught up in charismatic mess. But rest assured, they do have a position in the Kingdom of God, seated in heavenly places with Christ Jesus.

In these prayers over 90% of them are scripture. The others have scriptures tagged to the end of the prayer verses to ensure a response from the heavenly host. It is written: *I will hasten my word to perform it.*

I would also suggest those who want immediate breakthroughs that would have a permanent and lasting effect, that you would first clean your house. I have done deliverances going to people's houses to find out they had certain objects that would act as a device that would attract spirits and satanic attacks, spying, monitoring, etc. We have to be careful about buying African, Aztec, Egyptian, Roman, and Greek figurines, statues, masks, artifacts, jewelry, etc.

These are doorways including frogs, and spider's figurines. Pray and ask the Holy Spirit for wisdom on what to remove, burn, smash, and destroy. This also includes all Harry Potter books, movies, and accessories that some have bought their children. Now that you don't have to pray about it, just get rid of it.

Fasting and consecration incorporated with the reading of the prayers in this book will be a key factor in your freedom, breakthroughs, and deliverance. Seek God on what type of fast he leads you on, for whatever particular situation that you, your ministry, business, or church are up against. Follow the Holy Spirit's leading to the letter, no short cuts.

I know I'm giving orders like a military commander, but remember you're in a war against powers, principalities, and spiritual wickedness in high places. In Rev. 12:7-9, when there was war in heaven and satan fought against Michael and his angels and they got kicked out, they were in a state of war. And millions of years later there is still a state of war against mankind.

These prayers are two-fold; they both attack the powers of darkness in the air and their ground forces. Most of the warfare that we contend with is planned on the earth and executed from up in the second heaven.

This is the realm where witches and warlocks, sorcerers, and balaams plant their curses and send up their prayers, chants, etc. The enemy has altars in the heavens, with pots and caldrons with your family's name on them. And there are those from which family dedications were made by our ancestors. What's even more cunning, the devil uses weak people, those that can influence others in the church to execute their works of wickedness on behalf of the kingdom of darkness.

Some of us have been marked for destitution through witchcraft. All of these are planted curses against you through psychic prayers and astral projection.

There are spoken word curses, and psychic meditations that are released so that demons and satanic forces can take on the assignment of enforcing those thoughts and utterances.

The scary version of this all is that about 70% of the witchcraft being operated on you is from people that are within the four walls of the church. Not the workers of iniquity that come visit the church but those that have been there for sometimes years, that have infiltrated the ministry .

Church witches are disguised, anointed, and assigned by satan to take over, especially prayers. They use their prophetic gift to soothsay you into their web. These are black widows. It is written he is the anointed cherub that covereth.

Dr. Itola wrote an excellent book called "Witchcraft in the Church." I suggest all leaders read it.

2Cor. 11:14-15: And no marvel; for satan himself is transformed into an angel of light. Therefore it is no great thing if his ministers also be transformed as the ministers of righteousness; whose end shall be according to their works.

Psalm 10:4-10: The wicked, through the pride of his countenance, will not seek after God: God is not in all his thoughts. His ways are always grievous; thy judgments are far above out of his sight; as for all his enemies, he puffeth at them. He hath said in his heart, I shall not be moved; for I shall never be in adversity. His mouth is full of cursing and deceit and fraud; under his tongue is mischief and vanity.

He sitteth in the lurking places of the villages; in the secret places doth he murder the innocent; his eyes are privily set against the poor. He lieth in wait secretly as a lion in his den; he lieth in wait to catch the poor; he doth catch the poor, when he draweth him into his net. He croucheth, and humbleth himself, that the poor may fall by his strong ones.

The enemy already has an advantage over us as individuals, as leaders, and as a church. Take time out to study the scripture tags, to help increase your knowledge so that when you pray these prayers you will have a greater understanding so that your faith comes in agreement with the revelations and the word of God. If the Holy Ghost takes up in you, go for it, for the spirit knows our infirmity, and he will make intercessions for you!!

Be sure to repent and confess your faults and sins before you enter into battle, for His grace is sufficient. Remember, since the days of John the Baptist, the Kingdom suffereth violence and the violent take it by force. Be strong in the power of HIS might.

God bless,

The Author

Words to Live By!!

Sun Tzu quotes from the Art of War and biblical scriptures in which some of the scriptures are the words in Red spoken by Jesus Christ or Yeshua Hamashiah himself who is the greatest warrior of all mankind

1. Blitzkrieg: it is only one who is thoroughly acquainted with the waging of war who can thoroughly understand the profitable way of carrying it on.

2. If you know the enemy and know yourself, you need not fear the result of a hundred battles. If you know yourself, but not the enemy, for every victory gained you will also suffer defeat. If you know neither the enemy nor yourself, you will succumb in every battle.

3. The art of war teaches us to rely not on the likelihood of the enemy not coming, but on our own readiness to receive him; not on the chance of his not attacking, but rather on the fact that we have made our position unassailable.

4. In battle, there are not more than two methods of attack -- the direct and indirect; yet these two in combination give rise to an endless series of maneuvers. The direct and indirect lead on to each other in turn. It is like moving in a circle -- you never come to an end. Who can exhaust the possibilities of their combination?

5. Good fighters of old first put themselves beyond the possibility of defeat and then waited for an opportunity of defeating the enemy. To secure ourselves against defeat lies in our own hands, but the opportunity of defeating the enemy is provided by the enemy himself.

6. The experienced soldier, once in motion, is never bewildered. Once he has broken camp, he is never at a loss. Hence the saying: If you know the enemy and know yourself, and your victory will not stand in doubt; if you know Heaven and know Earth, you may make your victory complete.

7. When a warlike prince attacks a powerful state, his generalship shows itself in preventing the concentration of the enemies' forces. He overawes his opponents, and their allies are prevented from joining against him. Hence he does not strive to ally himself with all and sundry, nor does he foster the power of other states. He carries out his own secret designs, keeping his antagonists in awe. Thus he is able to capture their cities and overthrow their Kingdoms!!

8. From this series of war, we should learn that victories should be followed up and the defeated enemy be given no chance to recover.

9. All warfare is based on deception. Hence when able to attack, we must seem unable; when using our forces, we must seem inactive; when we are near, we must make the enemy believe that we are far away; we must make him believe we are near. Hold out baits to entice the enemy. Fein disorder and crush him.

1.) Matt. 11:12 (KJV) **12** And from the days of John the Baptist until now the kingdom of heaven suffereth violence, and the violent take it by force.

2.) Luke 11:17-20 (KJV) **17** But he, knowing their thoughts, said unto them, Every kingdom divided against itself is brought to desolation; and a house *divided* against a house falleth. **18** If Satan also be divided against himself, how shall his kingdom stand? because ye say that I cast out devils through Beelzebub. **19** And if I by Beelzebub cast out devils, by whom do your sons cast *them* out? therefore shall they be your judges. **20** But if I with the finger of

God cast out devils, no doubt the kingdom of God is come upon you.

3.) Col. 1:12-13 (KJV) **12** Giving thanks unto the Father, which hath made us meet to be partakers of the inheritance of the saints in light: **13** Who hath delivered us from the power of darkness, and hath translated *us* into the kingdom of his dear Son.

4.) Matt. 16:18-19 (KJV) And I say also unto thee, That thou art Peter, and upon this rock I will build my church; and the gates of hell shall not prevail against it. **19** And I will give unto thee the keys of the kingdom of heaven: and whatsoever thou shalt bind on earth shall be bound in heaven: and whatsoever thou shalt loose on earth shall be loosed in heaven.

5.) Rev. 12:10-11 (KJV) **10** And I heard a loud voice saying in heaven, Now is come salvation, and strength, and the kingdom of our God, and the power of his Christ: for the accuser of our brethren is cast down, which accused them before our God day and night. **11** And they overcame him by the blood of the Lamb and by the word of their testimony; and they loved not their lives unto the death.

6.) Acts 14:22 (KJV) **22** Confirming the souls of the disciples, *and* exhorting them to continue in the faith, and that we must through much tribulation enter into the kingdom of God.

7.) Mark 3:24-27 (KJV) And if a kingdom be divided against itself, that kingdom cannot stand. **25** And if a house be divided against itself, that house cannot stand. **26** And if Satan rise up against himself, and be divided, he cannot stand, but hath an end. **27** No man can enter into a strong man's house, and spoil his goods, except he will first bind the strong man; and then he will spoil his house.

8.) Matt. 13:41-43 (KJV) **41** The Son of man shall send forth his angels, and they shall gather out of his kingdom all things that offend, and them which do iniquity; **42** And shall cast them into a furnace of fire: there shall be wailing and gnashing of teeth. **43** Then shall the righteous shine forth as the sun in the kingdom of their Father. Who hath ears to hear, let him hear.

9.) 1 Cor. 4:20 (KJV) **20** For the kingdom of God *is* not in word, but in power.

10.) Mark 1:15 (KJV) And saying, The time is fulfilled, and the kingdom of God is at hand: repent ye, and believe the gospel.

11.) 2 Cor. 10:1-6 (KJV) **1** Now I Paul myself beseech you by the meekness and gentleness of Christ, who in presence *am* base among you, but being absent am bold toward you: **2** But I beseech *you*, that I may not be bold when I am present with that confidence, wherewith I think to be bold against some, which think of us as if we walked according to the flesh. **3** For though we walk in the flesh, we do not war after the flesh: **4** (For the weapons of our warfare *are* not carnal, but mighty through God to the pulling down of strong holds;) **5** Casting down imaginations, and every high thing that exalteth itself against the knowledge of God, and bringing into captivity every thought to the obedience of Christ; **6** And having in a readiness to revenge all disobedience, when your obedience is fulfilled.

12.) Isaiah 30:30 (KJV) **30** And the LORD shall cause his glorious voice to be heard, and shall shew the lighting down of his arm, with the indignation of *his* anger, and *with* the flame of a devouring fire, *with* scattering, and tempest, and hailstones.

13.) Luke 4:18-19 (KJV) **18** The Spirit of the Lord *is* upon me, because he hath anointed me to preach the gospel to the poor; he hath sent me to heal the brokenhearted, to preach deliverance to the captives, and recovering of sight to the blind, to set at liberty them that are bruised, **19** To preach the acceptable year of the Lord.

In life through all of our trials and triumphs the greatest thing that GOD has equipped those of us that are saved, is the dispensation of HIS GRACE!!!!! Through the constructing of this manual I have not only learned about the victory you can achieve through the praying of the word of God, but the LOVE of God that makes deliverance possible. It is HIS desire that we be set free from demonic and satanic oppression for whatever the cause!!!!

That is what Luke 4:18 is all about. I know some will disagree but to those of you that are bound by unseen forces that don't know which way to turn, or those of you that love God but your family has dedicated you to Satan to be his bride or his slave, or those of you that are oppressed cause a family member operates in witchcraft or has sold your soul for wealth and power, or those that are being raped or harassed by demons of the night, or those that are being oppressed with schizophrenia into suicide attempts, people spying on you through astral projection, demons cutting holes in your pockets through generational poverty, arrested development, drug addiction, prostitution, spoken word curses, psychic prayers, kadesh barnea cycles in life and ministry, demonic barriers of stagnation and backwardness through external and internal soul ties and other devices of satanic oppression, this book is for you !!

Most ministries don't deal with these matters of spiritual warfare and deliverance on this level, in most cases (or people) are ignored, given a lullaby and swept under rug. But it is high time that we dealt with these issues like Elisha in 2Kings 9, JESUS in Luke 11:20-22, Phillip did in Acts 8, and Paul in Acts 19!! It's time for the Body of Christ to have an Endtime Riot in Ephesus!!

The Bride of Christ needs to repent and quit committing adultery with Balaam and Jezebel and their Spiritual cohorts!!!! The Son of Man was manifest to destroy the works of the devil; this book is part of that manifestation, and yes these prayers were birth out through battle!!!! Enjoy the victories to come in the name of Jesus Christ. Amen!!!

Keep in mind that these prayers are aimed and directed at the powers and principalities and the demonic spirits that are deployed and at work in enforcing curses, not the people who send them or whom the devil is able to use in the earth realm. God is about love that is what Calvary is all about. In in-depth studies every scripture deals with destroying the works and the spirit that operates through its host (person) this is the Goal of these prayers in this book and the intention of my heart.

Remember, Pray these Prayers out loud!!!!

Pray as the Holy Spirit instructs you and seek out for someone to do some deliverance on you, if no one is available ask the Holy Spirit to purge you!!!!

If you pray these prayers, and fast as the Holy Spirit instructs you, and if your heart is right with God, and if you do not operate in iniquity or witchcraft of any form,

You will receive breakthrough after breakthrough!!!!

Sincerely,

The Author

Blitzkrieg

Father God in the name of Jesus Christ of Nazareth, Lord, we repent for the Kingdom of God has come nigh unto us. God, deliver me from all my transgressions according to Psalm 39:8. God, send fire 7 times hotter as in Dan. 3:19; to burn off our bonds as you burned the bonds off Shadrach, Meshach, Abednego . God, we confess the sins, trespasses, iniquities, rebellion, idolatry, passivity, unbelief, unforgiveness, gossip, loshon hora, sexual immorality, slander, false witness, lying tongue, wicked imagination, sowing discord, and not tithing consistently. Now God go through our blood line from cavalry to this very moment. Lord we confess the sins, the iniquities, the trespasses, and the ignorance and disobedience of ourselves, our foremothers and forefathers going back 42 generations according to Lev. 26:40-42. For you said if we shall confess our iniquity, and the iniquity of our fathers, with their trespass that they have trespassed against you, and that they also have walked contrary unto you, and that you have also walked contrary unto them, and have brought them (us) into the land of their enemies; if then their uncircumcised heart be humbled, and then they accept the punishment of their iniquity: then will I remember my covenant with Jacob and also my covenant with Isaac, and also my covenant with Abraham will I remember; and I will remember the land. Lord, we confess our sins and the sins of our fathers in the name of the Lord Jesus Christ.

God, even though this is a general confession, honor our faith according to your word. God, purge our blood line with the blood of Jesus Christ. We release confusion, chaos, destruction, panic, havoc, disasters, and blindness, upon every demonic confederacy policing our blood line, in the name of Jesus Christ. God, send your angels with everlasting chains according to Matt. 13:41-42 and Psalm 103:20, to bind up every strongman, every policing demon, every demonic enforcer, all demon drones, all imps that bring in military enforcement, demon reapers that down-load information in the spirit realm, winged shadow demons that are responsible for network communications, attacks, backlash, retaliation, sabotage and booby traps, skeleton lords, and all demonic door and gate keepers and we spoil their goods, according to Matt. 18:18, Mark 3:27, that would illegally reinstate curses to open and keep open door ways for attacks of affliction and oppression on our family, ministry, finances, property, possessions, inheritance, and destiny seeing it is a righteous thing for God to recompense tribulation to them that trouble you according to 2Thes 1:6.

Lord we take the Key of David and close every door at the point of entry in the name of Jesus Christ according to Rev. 3:7. God, we repent and ask that you break every curse including the curse of the Bastard in the name of Jesus Christ; for Gal 3:13 says Christ has redeemed us from the curse of the law, being made a curse for us: for it is written, cursed is everyone that hangeth from a tree, God, according to 1 John 1:7, 9. If we confess our sins you are faithful and just to forgive us and the Blood of Jesus Christ will cleanse us from all unrighteousness. Jesus send your blood, the same Blood that spilled on Calvary, through our bloodline like a tsunami tidal wave in the name of Jesus Christ. Now God, send fire 7 times hotter even as fire and brimstone destroyed Sodom and Gomorrah according to Gen 19:24; let fire and brimstone rain and destroy every family curse and works of witchcraft, and divination going through our Blood line. God, send Angels with everlasting chains to bind up every demon of legalism operating, according to 2Pet 2:4. Jesus hear my prayer Oh Lord, and give ear to my cry. Lord, as we sound the shofar, sound that grand tekoa in heaven; for our God shall fight for us according to Neh 4:20; and as we shout the sword of the Lord and of Gideon. Jesus set every man's sword against his fellow according to Judges 7:20-22. God, open up your armory, and bring forth your weapons of indignation, according to Jer 50:25; call together your archers against Babylon and all of our enemies: all ye that bend the bow, camp against it round about. Let none therefore escape: recompense her according to all she hath done, do unto her for she have been proud against the Lord, against the Holy One of Israel, therefore shall her young men fall in the streets, and all her men of war shall be cut off in that day, saith the Lord. For the Lord is a man of war and the Lord is his name.

For the weapons of warfare are not carnal but mighty through God by the pulling down of strong holds, casting down imaginations and everything that is high-minded, that exalt itself against the knowledge of God. In the name of the Lord Jesus Christ, we pull down every strong hold on our family, finances, property, business, ministry, and destiny, we spoil the goods of every strong man, for Lord you spoiled principalities and powers and brought them to an open shame, Lord be a spoiler to those who have spoiled us according to Isaiah 33:1, Ezekiel 39:10; for no weapon that is formed against us shall prosper and every tongue that rises up against us though shall condemn, deliver me oh Lord, from the evil man: preserve me from the violent, which imagine mischiefs in their heart; continually they are gathered together for war; keep me from the snares they have laid for me, and the gins of the workers of Iniquity; let the wicked fall into their own nets, whilst that I withal escape. Yet (God) I destroyed the Amorite from before them, whose height was like the height of the cedars, and he was strong as the oaks; yet (God) I destroyed his fruit from above, and his roots from beneath. God destroy every root and fruit of every Amorite in our life and our entire bloodline in the name of Jesus Christ according to Amos 2:9.

Lord as we pray, help us as you helped Moses and Joshua and the children of Israel to smite the 31 kings according to Josh Chap.12, God, release a blitzkrieg upon our oppressors in the name of Jesus Christ; for Great is our Lord and of great power; his understanding is infinite, the Lord lifteth up the meek: he casteth the wicked down to the ground. Praise ye the Lord, praise God in his sanctuary: praise him in the firmament of his power, praise him for his mighty acts, praise him according to his excellent greatness. For God you said out of your own mouth that there is nothing too hard for you.

Trust ye in the Lord forever: for in the Lord JE-HO'-VAH is an everlasting strength, for his Kingdom is an everlasting kingdom and all dominions shall serve and obey him according to Dan 7:27.
 The Lord is my rock, and my fortress, and my deliverer; my God, my strength, in whom I trust; my buckler, and the horn of my salvation, and my high tower. I will call upon the Lord who is worthy to be praised; so shall I be saved from mine (our) enemies, for every valley shall be exalted, and every mountain and hill made low; and the crooked shall be made straight, and the rough places plain. And the glory of the Lord shall be revealed, and all flesh shall see it together: for I am HE that liveth, and was dead; and behold, I am alive forever more, and have the keys of hell and of death, for the mouth of the Lord hath spoken it; God!!!!! Send your end time angels to be an enemy to our enemies and an adversary to our adversaries. Send hornets to drive out the Hivite, the Canaanite, and the Hittite from before thee. Send Angels with the sword of the Lord with vengeances and Judgment to bind up, smite and consume, Lilith that screeching owl, Cockatrice, the satyr, leviathan and every demonic prince with the edge of the sword and utterly destroy all the souls of every demonic confederacy of affliction and oppression sent at me, my family, finances, property and all that pertains to me according to Zeph 1:2-3. For behold, the whirlwind of the Lord goeth forth with fury, a continuing whirlwind: it shall fall with pain upon the head of the wicked. The fierce anger of the Lord shall not return, until he hath done it, and until he hath performed the intents of his heart. For the chariots of God are twenty thousands, and thousands of angels, and the Lord is with them. God, send warrior angels to break down all hedges, uproot all of the enemies' strong holds and bring them to ruins in the name of Jesus Christ according to Psalm 89:40.

All the horns of the wicked shall be cut off; but the horns of the righteous shall be exalted. Hashem cut off the spirit of the princes and was terrible to the kings of the earth according to Isaiah 34:12. For my God is a King of old, working salvation in the midst of the earth; thou didst divide the sea by his strength, thou breakest the heads of Leviathan in pieces and gavest him to be meat in the name of Jesus Christ. God, make hast for our help, let them be confounded and consumed that are adversaries to my soul, let them be covered with reproach and dishonor that seek my hurt. And those that seek our soul to destroy it shall go into the lower parts of the earth; they shall fall by the sword and be a portion for foxes. Let not the foot of pride come against us, and let not the hand of the wicked remove me. They are the workers of iniquity fallen; they are cast down and shall not be able to rise. Now is come salvation, and strength, and the Kingdom of our God, and the power of his Christ: for the accuser of the brethren is cast down, and they overcame him by the BLOOD OF THE LAMB and the word of their testimony. For thou art my rock and my fortress, therefore, for thy name's sake lead me and guide me, pull me out of the net that they have hid privily for me, for thou art my strength. In my distress I called upon the Lord, and cried unto my God. He heard my voice out of his Holy temple, and my (our) cry came before him, even into his ears. Then the earth shook and trembled; the foundations also of the hills moved and were shaken because of his wroth. For the Lord also thundered in the heavens, and the Highest gave his voice; hail stones and coals of fire. Yea, he sent out his arrows, and scattered them; and he shot lightning, and discomforted them. Thou hast also given me the necks of mine enemies that I might destroy them that hate me; they cried but there was none to save them; even unto the Lord, but he answered them not.

Let them be confounded and put to shame that seek after my soul; let them be turned back and brought to confusion that devise my hurt; let them be as chaff before the wind; and let the angel of the Lord chase them. Let their way be dark and slippery and let the angel of the Lord chase them; let their way be dark and slippery and let the angel of the Lord persecute them. For without cause have they hid their net in a pit, which without cause they have digged for my soul. Let destruction come upon them unawares, and let his net that he hid catch himself, into that very destruction let him fall. And my soul shall rejoice and be joyful in the Lord.

Be thou exalted, Hashem, in thine own strength: so we will sing and praise thy power. Behold the eye of the Lord is upon them that fear him, upon them that hope in his mercy. Blessed be the Lord, who hath not given us as a prey to their teeth. Our soul is escaped as a bird out of the snare of the fowler; the snare is broken, and we are escaped. Lord, we thank you for breaking every snare in the name of Jesus Christ. I shall not die but live to declare the works of the Lord. For the Lord hath redeemed Jacob, and ransomed him from the hand of him that was stronger than he. For thou art my battle axe and weapons of war: for with thee will I break in pieces the nations, and with thee I will destroy kingdoms; and I will also break in pieces the horse and his rider; and with thee I will break in pieces the chariot and his rider, and a sword is upon the liars; and they shall dote: a sword is upon her mighty men; and they shall be dismayed and there stronghold overthrown according to Jer 50:35-40.

Bow the heavens, O Lord, and come down: touch the mountains and they shall smoke. Cast forth lighting and scatter them; shoot out thine arrows and destroy them; send thine hand from above, rid me, and deliver me out of great waters, from the hand of strange children; whose mouth speaketh vanity, and their right hand, is the right hand of falsehood. Let mine adversaries be clothed with shame, and let them cover themselves with their own confusion. As with a mantle, let the extortioner catch all that he hath; and let the strangers spoil his labor. Let there be none to extend mercy unto him, and as he loved cursing, so let it come unto him; and as he delighteth not in blessing, so let it be far from him, as he clothed himself with cursing like a garment, so let it come into his own bowels like water, and like oil into his bones. Let it be unto him as a garment which covereth him, and for a girdle where with he is girded continually.

Let this be the reward of mine (our) adversaries from the Lord, and of them that speak evil against my (our) soul. For I have faith in God and I speak unto every demonic mountain in my (our) life be thou removed and be thou cast into the sea; for Behold I am (God) against thee, O destroying mountain saith the Lord, which destroyed all the earth: and I will stretch out mine hand upon thee, and roll thee down from the rocks, and will make thee a burnt mountain. And they shall not take of thee a stone for a corner, nor a stone for foundations; but thou shalt be desolate forever, saith the Lord. And I will call for a sword against him throughout all my mountains, saith the Lord God: every man's sword shall be against his brother. And I will plead against him with pestilence and with blood; and I will rain upon him and upon his bands; and upon the many people that are with him, an overflowing rain of great hail stones, fire and brimstones, Thus will I (God) magnify myself and sanctify myself; for many sorrows shall be to the wicked: but he that trusteth in the Lord, mercy shall compass him about.

And behold, there was war in heaven, and Michael and his angels fought against the dragon; and the dragon fought with his angels and prevailed not. God send Michael and his angels to rage war on our behalf in the name of Jesus Christ; for God spared not the angels that sinned, but cast them down to Tartartus, and delivered them into chains of darkness, to be reserved unto judgment. God every demonic prince and his host that has come against us, bind them in everlasting chains and take them to Tartartus according to Jude 1:6 and then that wicked shall be revealed, whom the Lord shall consume with the spirit of his mouth and destroy with the brightness of his coming. In that day the Lord with his great and strong sword shall punish Leviathan the piercing serpent, even Leviathan that crooked serpent; and he shall slay the dragon that is in the sea. We put the 5 Kings of oppression in the cave according to Josh. 10:23-25. For the Son of man shall send forth his angels, and they shall gather out of his kingdom all things that offend, and them which do iniquity; and shall cast them into a furnace of fire: and there shall be wailing and gnashing of teeth.

Woe unto them that devise iniquity, and they that work evil upon their beds! When the morning is light they practice it, because it is in the power of their hand. For thou shalt not suffer a witch, warlock, necromancer, enchanter, satanist and sorcerer to live; and now behold the hand of the Lord is upon thee and thou shalt be blind not seeing for a season. Lord Jesus we smite the third eye with blindness according 2Kings 6:18. Lord frustrate their works according to Isaiah 44:25, Psalm 2:9. In the name of Jesus Christ, we bind and curse the success of Hecate and the power of all witchcraft, voodoo, necromancy, divination, push pin dolls, spells, conjurations, incantations, root workings, hexes, vexes, amulets, spoken curses, prophetic witchcraft prayers and revelation for attacks, chanting curses on a pentagram, and psychic mind control of every sort, level, order, rank, time and place we curse it to death; like Jesus cursed the fig tree according to Mark 11:14, 20-21. For God in Isaiah 41:10-13, you said fear thou not; for I am with thee; be not dismayed; for I am thy God; I will strengthen thee; yea, I will help thee; yea I will uphold thee with the right hand of my righteousness. Behold all they that were incensed against thee shall be ashamed and confounded: they shall be as nothing; and they that strive with thee shall perish. Thou shalt seek them, and shalt not find them, even them that contend with thee: they that war against thee shall be as nothing, and as a thing of naught, for I the Lord thy God will hold thy right hand, saying unto thee. Fear not; I will help thee. For Jesus you said every kingdom divided against itself is brought to desolation; and every city or house divided against itself shall not stand. Father in the name of Jesus Christ send Michael and his angels to wage war and to drive out, divide, and desolate every kingdom of darkness, and the strong holds that the strong men have over our house, clan and family blood line by the finger of God and the power of your everlasting Kingdom according to Luke 11:20-22.

Now Father we release the Spirit of Elijah to prophesy doom and annihilation against the kingdom of Ahab and Jezebel according to 1Kings 22:19-24; and we release the Spirit of Elisha to instruct the prophets to anoint the end time Jehu's to be relentless and to release a double portion of that spirit to combat against Jezebel and the host in her kingdom according to 2Kings 9:6-10:14. We call forth eunuchs to throw her down from her high place to be trodden by horses according 2Kings 9:33; and we release the dogs of Jezreel to eat her flesh works. God, let the dogs out according to 2Kings 9:36-37, in the name of Jesus Christ. Lord open up the kennels of heaven and send the dogs of Jezreel to hunt down and to chew up and destroy all Jezebelic prayers, psychic prayers, well-meaning prayers that are not God's will for our lives, all mind manipulation, group controlling witchcraft and its works, in our churches, and in our lives. We break covenant, severe, cut, burn, blow up, undamn, annihilate and destroy all their works and break every 3-fold demonic cord with an everlasting fire. For our God is a consuming fire in the name of Jesus Christ according to 2Kings 9:22, Judges 16:9. Even as I have seen; they that plow iniquity, and sow wickedness, reap the same, by the blast of God they perish, and by the breath of his nostrils are they consumed according to Job 4:8-9. God send a blast upon him, and he shall hear a rumor, and return to his own land; and I will cause him to fall by the sword of his own land, according to Isaiah 37:7.

In the name of Jesus Christ, we come against falsehood, slander, speculation, character assassination, and spiritual projection and we reverse and return every undermining effort against our character in the name of Jesus Christ according to Psalm 144:11. Lord we curse and bind up Pyrox, Alato and release judgment on all remote viewing and traveling, and astral projection according to Ezek 13:20, Ecc 12:6, Josh 10:19. For the eyes of the wicked shall fail, and they shall not escape, according to Job 11:20. Father, grant not, O Lord the desires of the wicked, further not his wicked device lest they exalt themselves. As for the head of those that compass me about, let the mischief of their own lips cover them.
Let burning coals fall upon them: let them be cast into the fire; into deep pits that they raise not again. And the Lord shall put all these curses upon thine enemies and on them that hated thee which

persecuted thee. God every curse that was spoken or conjured against every area of our lives and on our family, that is lingering in the atmosphere, God as you gave commandment to Balaam to bless as he was sent curse, Lord Jesus Christ reverse every curse sent to us and our forefathers and turn it into a blessing in the name of Jesus Christ according to Num. 23:20-24.

Lord God of Abraham, Isaac, and Israel, let it be known this day that thou art God in Israel, and that I am thy servant, and that I have done all these things at thy word. Oh Lord, hear me that this people may know that thou art God, and that thou hast turned their heart back again. For behold I come with fire, and with his chariots like a whirlwind, to render his anger with fury, and his rebuke with flames of fire. God send fire as in Acts 19:19; to burn up the curious arts and to destroy the works of witchcraft released upon our lives since birth. Lord, bless us and keep us in the name of Jesus Christ according to Num 6:22-27, Psalm 121. God, send fire upon Moab and it shall devour the palaces of Kiroth; and Moab shall die in tumult (desolation and destruction) with shouting and with the sound of the shofar, and I will cut off the judge from the midst thereof, and I will slay the princes (chief rulers) thereof with him sayeth the Lord.

God according to Job 12:13-19, with you is wisdom and strength, counsel and understanding. Behold you breaketh down, and it shall not be built again; he shutteth up a man, and there can be no opening. Behold he withholden the waters, and they dry up; he sendeth them out, and they overturn the earth. With him is strength and wisdom: and the deceived and the deceiver are his. He leadeth counselors away spoiled, and maketh the judges fools. He looseth the bond of kings, and girdeth their loins with girdle. He leadeth princes away spoiled, and overthroweth the mighty. Thus saith the Lord, even the captives of the mighty shall be taken away, and the prey of the terrible shall be delivered: for I will contend with him that contendeth with thee; and I will save thy children; and I will feed them that oppress thee with their own flesh; and they shall be drunken with their own blood and all flesh shall know that I the Lord, I am thy Savior and thy Redeemer the mighty one of Jacob. So shout now and let the high praises of God be in our mouth and a two-edged sword in our hand, to bind their kings with chains, and there nobles with fetters of irons, to execute upon them the judgment written: this honor has all his saints. Praise the Lord for his mercy endureth forever.

I make a decree, that in every dominion, men tremble and fear before the God of Daniel: for he is the living God, and steadfast forever, and his kingdom that which shall not be destroyed, and his dominion shall be even unto the end. He delivereth and rescueth, and he worketh signs and wonders in heaven and in earth, who hath delivered Daniel from the power of the lions. God deliver us and our family through signs and wonders in the name of Jesus Christ. Now God I thank you, for in Lev. 26:6-9, You said, I will give peace in the land, and ye shall lie down, and none shall make you afraid: and I will rid evil beasts out of the land neither shall their sword go through your land. And you shall chase your enemies, and they shall fall by the sword. For I will have respect unto you, and make you fruitful, and multiply you, and establish my covenant with you. Hear diligently my speech oh God and my declaration with your ears according to Job 13:17 and I decree and declare this according Jer. 1:11. For the LORD hath broken forth upon mine enemies before me, as the breach of waters. Therefore he called the name of that place Baalperazim. God, we thank you for breaking through the enemies' strongholds on our behalf as you did for David.

And Lord, we thank you for the power of your Kingdom, for it is an everlasting Kingdom and it rules over every dominion; and we thank you for the Blood that was shed on Calvary. Oh God, in the name of Yeshua Hamashiah, cover us in your blood according to Exodus 12:13 in the name of Jesus Christ. Amen.

Commanding War in the Morning

Give ear to my words, O LORD, consider my meditation. Hearken unto the voice of my cry, my King, and my God: for unto thee will I pray. My voice shalt thou hear in the morning, O LORD; in the morning will I direct my prayer unto thee, and will look up.

Father God, in the name of Jesus Christ, we command the morning and the day spring to know its place, to rip up from top to bottom and destroy every invisible barrier of wickedness released from the second heaven that is, stopping, blocking, and delaying the release of our blessings that God has ordained for our life.

We command the morning according to Job 38:12-13; to smash and destroy every pot, every caldron that has my name, and my family's entire blood line written on it in the name of Jesus Christ.

We command the morning to take the ax of God, to cut off the heads of every python and evil serpent that has initiated, and released commands to program shame, disgrace, and poverty over our lives, and into our future in the name of Jesus Christ.

We command the morning, the day spring, the sun, the moon, and the stars, to take the ax of God and to continually chop up and destroy every 3-fold cord of mammon, poverty, and fear over our lives in the name of Jesus Christ according to Judges 15:14. God annihilate them by fire according Gen 19:24, 27.

We command the morning to destroy every power that is used to delay my success and the dayspring to know its place to cancel and destroy every power assigned to stop my success in the name of Jesus Christ.

We command the day spring to know its place to frustrate, to shake and release confusion upon all the works of wickedness of every confederacy of every person releasing demons and evil spirits sent to delay our blessings. God, we command the morning to break and release us, to erase, blot out, and remove our name with the blood of the Lamb from the book of poverty, sickness, defeat, stagnation, and shame in the name of Jesus Christ.

We command the morning to close every door at the point of entry, to bind, and lock up in fetters and chains every python, every evil spirit and demon released that has come through our blood line in the name of Jesus Christ.

We command the day spring to know its place to bind up every strong man, every spirit help, and every spirit guide, and to spoil their goods according to Mark 3:27, Num 14:9, and Psalm 68:17. We command the dayspring to know its place, to shake out wickedness from the ends of the earth that have been frustrating and hindering our blessings.

We command the sun, moon and the stars to send fire to destroy every curse, every hidden curse, every stubborn curse, every iron-like curse, and every ju ju. We release warrior angels with everlasting chains of darkness, to bind up every wicked spirit, every demon, every evil angel that has been sent to hinder, stagnate, sabotage and to paralyze our breakthroughs in our health, prosperity, and deliverance in the name of Jesus Christ, according 2Pet. 2:4, Job 14:17, Psalm 103:20, and Matt 13:41-42.

God, we command the morning according to Job 38:12-13, and the dayspring to know its place to break and return every curse of every sort, level, order, rank, time, and place and turn it into a blessing according to Neh 13:2, 2Kings 2:20-22.

We command the morning to bring healing and restoration to the foundation of our life, We command the dayspring to know its place, to pour out salt from the third heaven, salt from the throne room of God to dissolve every curse over our mind, body, spirit, soul and blood line according 2Kings 2:20-22.

Lord, open up the Heavens and pour out the blessings of the Lord which maketh rich and adddeth no sorrow. Lord, we repent for any disobedience that have brought blockages in our life. God, cause the dayspring to know its place, and to bring the healing salt of heaven into the foundation of our life.

We command the morning to stop, block, reverse, and return every form of hexes, vexes, stubborn curses, hidden curses, chants, meditations, sorcery, incantations, conjurations, hoodoo, voodoo, charismatic witchcraft and homemade witchcraft sent at us in the night seasons. God paralyze, veto and render every satanic plot, purpose, plan and strategy null and void according to Isaiah 19:14-16, Psalm 7:9.

God, overturn, and return, and seal every spiritual effect into the very bowels of the senders in the name of Jesus Christ according to Psalm 109:17-19, Psalm 79:12, and 1Kings 2:44.

We command the morning, the sun, the moon and the stars to lock up and erase with the blood of Jesus Christ, every witchcraft handwriting and ordinance of every sort, level, order, rank, time and place, that have brought stagnation and limitations into our lives according to Isaiah 44:25. We command fire to destroy these invisible barriers in the name of Jesus Christ according Jer 49:27, 50:15.

O LORD, be gracious unto us; we have waited for thee: be thou their arm every morning, our salvation also in the time of trouble.

We command the morning to locate and send fire from the throne room of God to destroy every satanic altar and every astral altar that is in the second heavens.

We command the morning to destroy every curse, every hidden curse that has been planted and programmed on these altars in the heavens. We curse the power, wisdom and success of ever satanic prophecy, chant, thought, meditation and ritual in the name of Jesus Christ, like Jesus cursed the fig tree according to Mark 11:14, 20.

We command the dayspring to know its place and shake wickedness out of the heavens and from ends of the earth; and God send a blast from the breath of your nostrils according to Job 4:8-9.

We command the morning to reject every iron-like (3-fold cord) curses of sickness, poverty, stagnation, procrastination, backwardness, and stalemate that have been planted in the heavens according to Judges 16:12, Neh 13:2, and 2Kings 2: 20-22.

We command the morning to release the whirlwind of the Lord and the fierce anger of the Lord according to Jer 30:22-24 to execute HIS judgment and the intents of HIS heart.

We command the morning and the day spring to know its place, to deprogram, cough up, reject, cancel, veto, and make null in void all wickedness that was programmed in the heavens over my star, in the night season, and to release the blessings, abundance, grace, and favor on our life in the name of Jesus Christ.

We command the morning, to cause to come down from you the rain, the former rain, and the latter rain in the first *month*. And the floors shall be full of wheat, and the fats shall overflow with wine and oil. And I will restore to you the years that the locust hath eaten, the canker worm, and the caterpillar, and the palmerworm.

My great army which I sent among you; and ye shall eat in plenty, and be satisfied, and praise the name of the LORD your God.

We command the morning and the day spring to know its place to locate, uncover, discover, revive, and make alive all hidden and buried potentials caused by unforeseen circumstances, throughout our life in the name of Jesus Christ.

We speak life to every gift, talent, prophecy, and promise that God has ordained for our life. Lord, we thank you; we give you the glory and honor, and we give you the praise for the transition in our lives according to Gen 39:2-3, in the name of Jesus Christ. Amen!!

Prayer Releasing the Wrath of God

Father God in the name of Jesus Christ we repent from all sins and iniquities and also the iniquities of our fathers; and God we ask that if we are not right in the sight of all heaven, we ask that you correct us and not hear this prayer.

For you said: Let all bitterness, and wrath, and anger, and clamor, and evil speaking, be put away from you, with all malice: And be ye kind one to another, tenderhearted, forgiving one another, even as God for Christ's sake hath forgiven you.

Now the works of the flesh are manifest, which are these: adultery, fornication, uncleanness, lasciviousness, Idolatry, witchcraft, hatred, variance, emulations, wrath, strife, seditions, heresies, envying, murders, drunkenness, revelings, and such like: of the which I tell you before, as I have also told you in time past, that they which do such things shall not inherit the kingdom of God.

But fornication, and all uncleanness, or covetousness, let it not be once named among you, as becometh saints; neither filthiness, nor foolish talking, nor jesting, which are not convenient: but rather the giving of thanks.

For this ye know, that no whoremonger, nor unclean person, nor covetous man, who is an idolater, hath any inheritance in the kingdom of Christ and of God.

Let no man deceive you with vain words: for because of these things cometh the wrath of God upon the children of disobedience. Be not ye therefore partakers with them. For ye were sometimes darkness, but now are ye light in the Lord: walk as children of light.

But the LORD is the true God; he is the living God, and an everlasting king: at his wrath the earth shall tremble, and the nations shall not be able to abide his indignation.

Thy right hand, O LORD, is become glorious in power: thy right hand, O LORD, hath dashed in pieces the enemy. And in the greatness of thine Excellency thou hast overthrown them that rose up against thee: thou sentest forth thy wrath, which consumed them as stubble.

And with the blast of thy nostrils the waters were gathered together, the floods stood upright as an heap, and the depths were congealed in the heart of the sea.

The enemy said, I will pursue, I will overtake, I will divide the spoil; my lust shall be satisfied upon them; I will draw my sword, my hand shall destroy them. Thou didst blow with thy wind, the sea covered them: they sank as lead in the mighty waters.

God, we release this wrath upon every type, level, order, rank, time and place against every form and work of witchcraft and charismatic witchcraft targeting our life that is designed to pursue and over take us, and divide us for a spoil in the name of Jesus Christ.

God, we ask that you root them out of their land in your anger and wrath and great indignation in the name of Jesus Christ according to Duet. 29:28.

Because he hath oppressed and hath forsaken the poor; because he hath violently taken away an house which he buildeth not; surely he shall not feel quietness in his belly, he shall not save of that which he desired.

There shall none of his meat be left; therefore shall no man look for his goods. In the fullness of his sufficiency he shall be in straits: every hand of the wicked shall come upon him.

When he is about to fill his belly, God shall cast the fury of his wrath upon him, and shall rain it upon him while he is eating. He shall flee from the iron weapon, and the bow of steel shall strike him through. It is drawn, and cometh out of the body; yea, the glittering sword cometh out of his gall: terrors are upon him.

In the name of Jesus Christ we release the wrath of God in this scripture verse against every witch, warlock, enchanter, Satanists, Balaams, Jezebels, voodoo doctors, hoodoo practitioners, and against all their underlings, assistants, attendants, and group participants and workers of charismatic witchcraft that have targeted us for attacks and for a spoil in the name of Jesus Christ according to Job 20:19-24.

How oft the candle of the wicked is put out! And how oft cometh their destruction upon them! God distributeth sorrows in his anger.

They are as stubble before the wind and as chaff that the storm carrieth away. God layeth up his iniquity for his children: he rewardeth him, and he shall know it.

His eyes shall see his destruction, and he shall drink of the wrath of the Almighty. For what pleasure hath he in his house after him, when the number of his months is cut off in the midst?

God, let this be the portion of all the workers of iniquity who have persecuted our soul without cause. Let your wrath be the breakfast, lunch, and dinner to everyone who was hired or prompted to curse us. God, let your wrath rest upon those who have put an open bounty on us in the name of Jesus Christ.

Let your wrath be the dwelling place of those who have volunteered to attack us, that are seeking promotion, wealth and power from Jezebel, and satan in the name of Jesus Christ.

Thine hand shall find out all thine enemies: thy right hand shall find out those that hate thee. Thou shalt make them as a fiery oven in the time of thine anger: the LORD shall swallow them up in his wrath, and the fire shall devour them.

Their fruit shalt thou destroy from the earth, and their seed from among the children of men. For they intended evil against thee: they imagined a mischievous device, which they are not able to perform.

Therefore shalt thou make them turn their back, when thou shalt make ready thine arrows upon thy strings against the face of them. Be thou exalted, LORD, in thine own strength: so will we sing and praise thy power.

God we bless you and praise you for the whole earth is filled with your glory; the whole earth is filled your glory, and we magnify your name; we give you the glory in the name of Yeshua Hamashiah. Amen.

Prayer to Destroy Satanic Databases

Father God in the name of Jesus Christ of Nazareth, we ask that you send fire heaven according to Amos 2:2-3 to burn and destroy every satanic data bases and main frames, books, files that contain information on me, my future, my past and present, my family and family blood line in the name of Jesus Christ.

We take the AXE of God and chop down all main frames, up links, and release Trojan bombs covered in the Blood of Jesus Christ into every operating system containing my files, we release viruses and a system crash, information contamination, meltdown, and destroy all information storage systems of every sort, level, order, rank, time and place in the name of Yeshua Hamashiah.

We release a tsunami title wave of the Blood of Jesus Christ into every operating system and search engine that is trying to locate and upload information on my past, present, and future, and destiny;
We release viruses, backdoor worms, Trojan spies, covered in the blood of Jesus Christ to destroy, destroy, destroy, all disks, files, books, thumb drivers, and every bit of information that has been stored on our past, present, and future.

God destroy with fire all information stored in caldrons and astral altars according to Gen. 19:24, 27.

We release fire from heaven, the same fire and brimstone that destroyed Sodom and Gomorrah, to destroy all information stored in the memory banks of all the workers of iniquity, demonic aids, and informants, and Jezebelic confederacies according to Isaiah 19:14-15, Isaiah 14:10, Num. 14:9.

We break and curse the power, wisdom and the success of every curse, chants, prayers, decrees, meditations and prophetic revelations, hand writings and ordinances, psychic channeling from the grave, of every sort, level, order, rank, time and place that has monitored our foundation in the name of Jesus Christ according to Mark 11:14, 20.

The heathen are sunk down in the pit that they made: in the net which they hid is their own foot taken. The LORD is known by the judgment which he executeth: the wicked is snared in the work of his own hands in the name of Jesus Christ:

We release panic, havoc, chaos, destruction, mayhem, confusion, on every individual, group, gathering and confederacy in the name of Jesus Christ according to Judges 7:20-22, 2Chron. 20:22-25, Jer. 51:58;

We break, burn, and destroy the power of every 3-fold cord alliance according to Judges 15:14, Psalm 2:3, that has knowingly and unknowingly formed and that would try to regroup itself;

We release confusion, paranoia, Alzheimer's, destitution and memory loss on every individual, group, gathering, that are attacking my life, my future, my family, health, finances, destiny and all that pertains to me in the name of Jesus Christ according to Isaiah 19:14-16; Isaiah 14:10.

We speak annihilation to their fortress and protection according to Psalm 89:40, Amos 2:2-3, Num. 14:9; and we release the angels of the Lord according to Jude 1:6, Psalm 103:20, Psalm 68:17 to lock up in fetters and everlasting chains, every satanic gate keeper, every demonic enforcer, evil angel, dark angel that is in the atmosphere that's sent to download, trace, follow, report, police, gather and upload new information in the name of Jesus Christ.

Lord, we give you the praise and we give you the honor, we release confusion, and backwardness in the minds of all satanic programmers that would try to retrieve any information and investigate my past and my future and destiny in the name of Jesus Christ.

We curse the works of their hands so that they cannot perform their enterprise in the name of Jesus Christ according to Matt. 13:41-42, Job 20:5-15.

And God, we thank you and praise your Holy names for you are the King of Kings and we bless you in the name of Yeshua Hamashiah. Amen.

Warfare Prayer against Star Hunters and Astral Enforcers

Father God in the name of Jesus Christ, we ask, oh God, that you smite with blindness and confusion every star gazer, every star hunters, and astral enforcers that has been tracking and following my Star in the name of Jesus Christ according to Judges 7:20-22, Gen. 19:11, 2Kings 6:18.

For the pride of thine heart hath deceived thee, thou that dwellest in the clefts of the rock, whose habitation *is* high; that sayeth in his heart, who shall bring me down to the ground? Though thou exalt *thyself* as the eagle, and though thou set thy nest among the stars, thence will I bring thee down, sayeth the LORD; according to Obadiah 3-4.

God, destroy by fire every altar in the heavens and on the earth that has my name or my family's name written on it in the name of Jesus Christ according to 2Kings 23:15.

The altar also was rent, and the ashes poured out from the altar, according to the sign which the man of God had given by the word of the LORD according to 1Kings 13:5.

In the name of Jesus Christ let every astral enforcer be frustrated and confused that follows after my star to track my progress in the name of Jesus Christ; according to Isaiah 19:14-16, Isaiah 44:25, Matt. 13: 41-42, Isaiah 14:10.

We bind blindness, confusion, dysfunction and error around the sight, senses, and discernment around all spiritual locaters, and those that have the gift in the name of Jesus Christ according to 2Kings 6:18.

God, in the name of Jesus Christ, we ask that you take your mighty hands, oh God, and rip up, and smash every cage that has been formed to imprison my star since birth in the name of Jesus Christ. For God, you said in Isaiah 54:17: that no weapon that is formed against me shall prosper.

God we smite the evil eye and the third eye with blindness, cataracts, and glaucoma that has been giving access and revelation to those that monitor my star in the name of Jesus Christ according to 2Kings 6:18, Gen. 19:11.

We release confusion and malfunctions in their satellite and communication networks so they cannot locate me in the name of Jesus Christ, according to Gen. 11:7-8.

God let all the information that has been stored and filed in satanic data bases on my life; be located and destroyed by fire according to Gen. 19:24, 27, Jer. 49:27.

LORD God of hosts, the God of Israel, awake to visit all the heathen: be not merciful to any wicked transgressors in the name of Jesus Christ.

And ye shall overthrow their altars, and break their pillars, and burn their groves with fire; and ye shall hew down the graven images of their gods, and destroy the names of them out of that place.

God we ask that you destroy by fire everything planted in the earth and in the heavens, destroy by fire every curse, every ju ju, that has been set up to distract, delay, hinder, derail, and sabotage my life in the name of Jesus Christ according to Job 14:17, Acts 19:19, Rev. 20:10.

God, send your angels to hunt down and bind up every evil spirit and ancestral spirit in everlasting Chains in the name of Yeshua Hamashiah according to 2Pet. 2:4.

God, destroy by fire everything that has been used by every witch, wizard, necromancer, Jezebel, and sorcerer that has any part of my personal effects, or that came off my body. Oh God, destroy every barricade and barrier with eternal fire in the name of Jesus Christ according to Amos 2:2-3, Jer. 51:58, Rev. 20:10.

God, release shame, disgrace, confusion, and backwardness against every person and confederacy that's been delaying my miracles in the name of Jesus Christ.

God, we ask that you cancel and reverse every promotion of every satanic agent that has been planting curses in my star. God, every one that has made attempts to attack me, let them receive backwardness and demotion instead of prosperity and promotion in the name of Jesus Christ according to Jer. 49:16, Isaiah 44:25, Num. 24:11.

God, release fear, torment, panic, havoc, confusion, stagnation, and desolation upon their lives until they back off, renounce, and cancel their assignments that they have plotted against my life, health and destiny in the name of Jesus Christ.

I release the angels of the Lord to bind up and lock in fetters and chains every spirit help, and every spirit guide around every person sent to monitor, report, and plant wickedness in my star in the name of Yeshua Hamashiah, according to Matt. 18:18, Jude.1:6, Obd. 3-4, Isaiah 19:14-16; Num. 14:9; Psalm 75:10a, and Psalm 149:8-9.

God, you sealeth up the hand of every man; that all men may know your doings. God seal up every hand that has performed wickedness against my life in the name of Jesus Christ according to Job 37:7-8.

God, I break and release my star and my destiny from the grip of all household witchcraft and return it to the sender in the name of Jesus Christ according to Psalm 109:17-19.

God, I break and release my star from all hoodoo, voodoo, and satanic devices in the name of Jesus Christ according to 2Cor.10:4-5, Isaiah 10:27.

God, I break and release my star from all family oaths, dedications and covenants made through satanic and witchcraft rituals for wealth, power, success, and protection in the name of Jesus Christ.

We command annihilation and destruction of every cage, snare, and barrier of vagabond, wandering, and underachievement planted in my star, let these barriers of delay and hindrances be ripped up and destroyed by fire; according 2Cor. 10:4, Amos 2:2-3, Jer. 51:58.

For the day of the LORD is near upon all the heathen: as thou hast done, it shall be done unto thee; thy reward shall return upon thine own head; let this be the reward of every star hunter, informant, and astral enforcer in the name of Jesus Christ according to Matt. 13:41-42.

He made a pit, and dug it, and is fallen into the ditch which he made. His mischief shall return upon his own head, and his violent dealing shall come down upon his own fate.

In the name of Yeshua Hamashiah I bind up every star hunter, star gazer and astral informant and enforcer with deaf, dumb, blindness, and paralysis that is trying to amputate and cut off my blessings, even at the point of breakthrough in the name of Jesus Christ according to Matt. 18:18a.

The LORD hath heard my supplication; the LORD will receive my prayer. Let all mine enemies be ashamed and sore vexed: let them return and be ashamed suddenly.

God, send your warrior angels to locate, break loose and break free all the blessings that you have ordained for my life, that have been blocked, hindered, and delayed from their release, throughout my life in the name of Jesus Christ.

For God, you said in your word, and I will restore to you the years that the locust hath eaten, the cankerworm, and the caterpillar, and the palmerworm, my great army which I sent among you. And ye shall eat in plenty, and be satisfied, and praise the name of the LORD your God.

God, I thank you and praise you for your word and the Power of deliverance for upon mount Zion shall be deliverance, and there shall be holiness; and the house of Jacob shall possess their possessions.

And the house of Jacob shall be a fire, and the house of Joseph a flame, and the house of Esau for stubble, and they shall kindle in them, and devour them; and there shall not be *any* remaining of the house of Esau; for the LORD hath spoken *it*. Now God, we thank you for your word and we praise you for the manifestation of this prayer in the name of Jesus Christ. Amen.

Warfare Prayer against Astral Projection

Bow the heavens O Lord, and come down: touch the mountains and they shall smoke. Cast forth lighting, and scatter them; shoot out thine arrows, and destroy them; send thine hand from above, rid me, and deliver me out of great waters, from the hand of strange children; whose mouth speaketh vanity, and there right hand, is the right hand of falsehood.

Let mine adversaries be clothed with shame, and let them cover themselves with their own confusion, as with a mantle, let the extortioner catch all that he hath; and let the strangers spoil his labor, let there be none to extend mercy unto him, and as he loved cursing, so let it come unto him; and as he delighteth not in blessing, so let it be far from him; as he clothed himself with cursing like a garment, so let it come into his own bowels like water, and like oil into his bones.

Let it be unto him as a garment which covereth him, and for a girdle where with he is girded continually. Let this be the reward of mine (our) adversaries from the Lord, and of them that speak evil against my (our) soul.

Break thou the arm of the wicked and the evil man; seek out his wickedness till thou find none.

Woe unto the wicked! It shall be ill with him; for the reward of his hands shall be given him according to Isa 3:11. In the name of Jesus Christ we come against falsehood, slander, speculation, character assassination, and spiritual projection and we reverse and return every undermining effort against our character in the name of Jesus Christ according to Psalm 144:11.

The pride of thine heart hath deceived thee, thou that dwellest in the clefts of the rock, whose habitation is high; that sayeth in his heart, who shall bring me down to the ground? Though thou exalt thyself as the eagle, and though thou set thy nest among the stars, thence will I bring thee down, sayeth the LORD.

Lord, we curse and bind up Pyrox, Alato and every related spirit in this function and we release God's wrath and judgment on all remote viewing and traveling, and astral projection according to Ezek. 13:20, Ecc. 12:6, Josh. 10:19. Lord, we cut, chop, and burn the silver cord for you said in Psalm 2:3.

Let us break their bands asunder, and cast away their cords from us. For in Prov. 13:17, a wicked messenger shall fall into mischief, let the messengers of satan fall prey to their own mischief. For the eyes of the wicked shall fail, and they shall not escape, according to Job 11:20.

Father we curse the success of all mind control, thought projection and mind manipulation through astral projection in the name of the Lord Jesus Christ .

 God destroy the gateways through soul ties and every point of access that they use with heaping hot coals and fire and brimstones in mighty name of the Lord Jesus Christ.

God take your sword and strike, cut, chop, and severe the heads every Leviathan, every piercing serpent, and every crooked serpent with your sore and great and strong sword in the name of Yeshua Hamashiah according to Isa 27:1

Father, grant not O Lord the desires of the wicked, further not his wicked device lest they exalt themselves, as for the head of those that compass me about, let the mischief of their own lips cover them. Let burning coals fall upon them; let them be cast into the fire; into deep pits that they raise not again.

And the Lord shall put all these curses upon thine enemies and on them that hated thee which persecuted thee. They shall lie down in the dust and the worms shall cover them, and another dieth in the bitterness of their soul, ye shall be brought to the grave, and shall remain in a tomb in the name of Jesus Christ according to Job 21:25-32.

God, erase every mark that is used as a homing beacon for projectionist to spy and inform on us in the name of Jesus Christ. Now will I shortly pour out my fury upon thee, and accomplish mine anger upon thee; and I will judge thee according to thy ways, and will recompense thee for all thine abominations.

God, let the manifestation of your word locate and be upon those who work wickedness against our lives through astral projection in the name of Jesus Christ.

God, every curse that was spoken or conjured against every area of our lives and on our family, that is lingering in the atmosphere, and that was planted in the heavens, we return it to the sender and we bind it and seal it, we double seal it , and we triple seal it in there bowels in the name of Jesus Christ and thank you and we give you the praise   Amen.

Destroying the Works of Balaam, Son of Boer

Father God in the name of Jesus Christ, we repent for any sins and unforgiveness that would allow access for any curse to attach itself to us in the name of Jesus Christ according to 1John 1:7, 9; for if we confess our sins, he is faithful and just to forgive us and the blood of Jesus Christ will cleanse us from all unrighteousness.

God, we repent for the sins of our fathers in the name of Jesus Christ according to Lev. 26:40-42.

God, we renounce any ungodly covenants and oaths that I or my ancestors have made to any idols, demons, false religions, witchcraft powers, organizations, and satan in the name of Jesus Christ according to Prov. 28:13.

We renounce and destroy with fire any family dedications and contracts made to satan for wealth, power, and fame in the name of Jesus Christ.

We take the key of David and shut and seal every door, points of entry and access, even through the blood line going back 70 generations in the name of Jesus Christ according to Rev. 3:7.

The LORD hath heard my supplication; the LORD will receive my prayer. Let all mine enemies be ashamed and sore vexed; let them return and be ashamed suddenly in the name of Jesus Christ.

We curse the power, wisdom, knowledge, promotion and success of every person that was hired to curse us in the name of Jesus Christ according to Num. 24:11, Isaiah14:10, Isaiah 19: 14-16, Num. 14:9.

God, we release error, Alzheimers, confusion, backwardness, stagnancy, panic, havoc, fear, and torment to locate and bind itself to every person that would attempt to place any curses on my life in the name of Jesus Christ according to Judges 7:20-22, Exodus 14:27-28.

O LORD God of hosts, the God of Israel, awake to visit all the heathen: be not merciful to any wicked transgressors.

We release famine, poverty, destitution, catastrophe, backwardness, and demotion to locate and BIND itself according to Matt. 18:18 a, against every person in the natural and in the spirit, who would hire a Balaam to curse me in the name of Jesus Christ according to Num. 24:11, 1Kings 2:44.

We release the 10 plagues of Egypt to hunt down, locate and manifest itself upon every Balaam, person, group, confederacy, and coven in the name of Jesus Christ.

We lock it up in their bowels until they cease and desist from there chants, meditations and works in the name of Jesus Christ according to Psalm 109.

Let the plagues not cease from their pursuit until they have found their targets in the name of Jesus Christ according to Jer. 30:23-24.

Even as I have seen, they that plow iniquity, and sow wickedness, reap the same. By the blast of God they perish, and by the breath of his nostrils are they consumed. The roaring of the lion, and the voice of the fierce lion, and the teeth of the young lions, are broken. The old lion perisheth for lack of prey, and the stout lion's whelps are scattered abroad.

God, we command their spirit guides and spirit helps to be located and locked up in everlasting chains, and their protection and defenses to depart from them in the name of Jesus Christ according to Num. 14:9, Psalm 75:10a, Isaiah 14:10, Mic. 3:6 a,b,c.

We bind the spirit of impotency against their powers, omens, prophecies, and their works in the name of Jesus Christ according to Matt. 18:18a.

Deliver me from mine enemies, O my God: defend me from them that rise up against me. Deliver me from the workers of iniquity, and save me from bloody men in the name of Jesus Christ.

We take the hand of God and knock them down from their High place for, Though thou exalt thyself as the eagle, and though thou set thy nest among the stars, thence will I bring thee down, sayeth the LORD.

We curse the power and success of every negative prophetic and satanic utterances in the name of Jesus Christ, God let every word they speak fall flat to the ground, let every vision they have be one of error, confusion and delusion according to Gen. 19:11; Ezek. 13:7 a, b.

For the sin of their mouth and the words of their lips let them even be taken in their pride: and for cursing and lying which they speak. Consume them in your wrath; consume them that they may not be: and let them know that God ruleth in Jacob unto the ends of the earth.

We release the judgment of God as spoken by the mouth of Moses against the works, and anointing of Balaam that has come against our life, business, ministry, and destiny in the name of Jesus Christ.

Knowest thou not this of old, since man was placed upon earth, that the triumphing of the wicked is short, and the joy of the hypocrite but for a moment? Though his Excellency mounts up to the heavens, and his head reach unto the clouds.

Yet he shall perish for ever like his own dung: they which have seen him shall say where is he? He shall fly away as a dream, and shall not be found: yea, he shall be chased away as a vision of the night. The eye also which saw him shall see him no more; neither shall his place any more behold him.

We curse the success of every power that has been sent and released to stagnate, hinder, and halt my progress in the name of Jesus Christ.

We release Psalm 109 to locate and hunt down every word, thought, and deed and return it and bind it to the bowels of every Balaam, every sender, and confederacy in the name of Jesus Christ according to Matt. 13:41-42, Isaiah 44:24-25.

Behold, I will send a blast upon him, and he shall hear a rumor, and shall return to his own land; and I will cause him to fall by the sword in his own land. God send a blast upon on every Balaam and those that hired them in the name of Jesus Christ according to Job 4:8-9, Isaiah 37:7.

We release heavenly judgment and the almighty wrath of God in the name of Jesus Christ against every contract and agreement released on our life that has not been validated by the Lord Jesus Christ.

God, we ask that you take your finger of God to locate and remove by fire and the blood of Jesus Christ every mark that has been formed and planted in the heavens and in the earth that acts as a signal, or a beacon for workers of every sort of sorcery and witchcraft to release curses of every sort, level, order, rank, time and place upon us in the name of Jesus Christ.

The Son of man shall send forth his angels, and they shall gather out of his kingdom all things that offend, and them which do iniquity; and shall cast them into a furnace of fire; there shall be wailing and gnashing of teeth. Then shall the righteous shine forth as the sun in the kingdom of their Father.

God, we ask that your turn everything that was meant for evil, into a blessing in the name of Jesus Christ according to Neh. 13:2.

God, we ask that your pour out your salt from the heavens to locate, rain down and disintegrate every Curse that was planted in the heavens and in the earth against our life, family, health and finances in the name of Jesus Christ of Nazareth.

But I will sing of thy power; yea, I will sing aloud of thy mercy in the morning: for thou hast been my defense and refuge in the day of my trouble. Unto thee, O my strength, will I sing: for God is my defense, and the God of my mercy. O let not the oppressed return ashamed; let the poor and needy praise thy name.

Lord Jesus, we thank you for your word, for you watch over your word to perform it and bring it to pass; and God we thank you for forgiveness and full restoration, for you said surely we shall recover all; and God we give you the glory in Jesus name. Amen.

Warfare Prayer against Witchcraft

Be thou exalted, Hashem, in thine own strength: so we will sing and praise thy power. Behold the eye of the Lord is upon them that fear him, upon them that hope in his mercy. Blessed be the Lord, who hath not given us as a prey to their teeth. Our soul is escaped as a bird out of the snare of the fowler; the snare is broken, and we are escaped, Lord we thank you for breaking every snare in the name of Jesus; I shall not die but live to declare the works of the Lord. For the Lord hath redeemed Jacob, and ransomed him from the hand of him that was stronger than he.

For thou art my battle axe and weapons of war: for with thee will I break in pieces the nations, and with thee I will destroy kingdoms; and I will also break in pieces the horse and his rider; and with thee I will break in pieces the chariot and his rider, and a sword is upon the liars; and they shall dote: a sword is upon her mighty men; and they shall be dismayed and there stronghold overthrown according to Jer. 50:35-40.

Woe unto them that devise iniquity, and they that work evil upon their beds! when the morning is light they practice it, because it is in the power of their hand, for thou shalt not suffer a witch, warlock, necromancer, satanist and sorcerer to live, and now behold the hand of the Lord is upon thee and thou shalt be blind not seeing for a season, Lord Jesus we smite the third eye with blindness according 2Kings 6:18.

God, destroy every level of all workings of mind control, mind binding, and mind blinding in the name of Jesus Christ,

God, destroy all enchantments, spell binding, 3-fold cord spells destroy them with an everlasting fire in name of the Lord Jesus Christ.

Lord, frustrate their works according to Isaiah 44:25, Psalm 2:9; in the name of Jesus Christ: we bind and curse the success of Hecate and the power of all witchcraft, voodoo, necromancy, divination, push pin dolls, conjurations, incantations, root workings, hexes, vexes, amulets, spoken curses, prophetic witchcraft prayers and revelation for attacks, chanting curses on a pentagram, and psychic mind control of every sort, level, order, rank, time, and place, we curse it to death; like Jesus cursed the fig tree according to Mark 11:14, 20-21.

For God, in Isaiah 41:10-13, you said fear thou not; for I am with thee: be not dismayed; for I am thy God. I will strengthen thee; yea, I will help thee; yea I will uphold thee with the right hand of my righteousness. Behold, all they that were incensed against thee shall be ashamed and confounded; they shall be as nothing; and they that strive with thee shall perish. Thou shalt seek them, and shalt not find them, even them that contend with thee; they that war against thee shall be as nothing, and as a thing of naught, for I the Lord thy God will hold thy right hand, saying unto thee, Fear not; I will help thee.

For Jesus, you said Every kingdom divided against itself is brought to desolation; and every city or house divided against itself shall not stand: Father, in the name of Jesus Christ send Michael and his angels to wage war and to drive out, divide, and desolate every kingdom of darkness, and the strong holds that the strong men have, over our house, clan and family blood line by the finger of God and the power of your everlasting Kingdom in the name of Jesus Christ according to Luke 11:20-22.

God, destroy and cancel all assignments of ancestral debt collectors through witchcraft in the name of Jesus Christ. God, destroy with fire every ancestral covenant made through witchcraft in the name of Jesus Christ according to Gen. 19:24, 27, Acts 19:19.

In the name of Jesus Christ, we come against falsehood, slander, speculation, character assassination, and spiritual projection and we reverse and return every undermining effort against our character and destiny in the name of Jesus Christ according to Psalm 144:11.

The LORD tryeth the righteous; but the wicked and him that loveth violence his soul hateth. Upon the wicked he shall rain snares, fire and brimstone, and an horrible tempest: this shall be the portion of their cup.

Lord, we curse the wisdom, the power, and the success of Pyrox, Alato and release judgment on these demonic princes that rule the air waves according to 2Pet. 2:4.

We release disruption, confusion, backwardness, stagnation and missed coordinance on all remote viewing and traveling, and astral projection according to Ezek. 13:20, Ecc. 12:6, Josh. 10:19. We curse the power, wisdom and success of planting curses on astral altars in the heavenlies according to Prov. 6:15; for the eyes of the wicked shall fail, and they shall not escape, according to Job 11:20.

Father, grant not O Lord the desires of the wicked, further not his wicked device lest they exalt themselves, as for the head of those that compass me about, let the mischief of their own lips cover them. Let burning coals fall upon them: let them be cast into the fire; into deep pits that they raise not again. And the Lord shall put all these curses upon thine enemies and on them that hated thee which persecuted thee.

God, every curse that was spoken or conjured against every area of our lives and on our family, that is lingering in the atmosphere, God as you gave commandment to Balaam to bless as he was sent curse, Lord Jesus Christ reverse every curse sent to us and our fore fathers and turn it into a blessing in the name of Jesus Christ according to Neh. 13:2.

For behold, I come with fire, and with his chariots like a whirlwind, to render his anger with fury, and his rebuke with flames of fire, God send fire as in Acts 19:19; to burn up the curious arts and to destroy the works of witchcraft released upon our lives since birth, Lord, bless us and keep us in the name of Jesus Christ according to Num 6:22-27, Psalm 121.

God send fire upon Moab and it shall devour the palaces of Kiroth: and Moab shall die in tumult (desolation and destruction) with shouting and with the sound of the shofar, and I will cut off the judge from the midst thereof, and I will slay the princes thereof with him sayeth the Lord.

God according to Job 12:13-19; with you is wisdom and strength, counsel and understanding. Behold you breaketh down, and it shall not be built again; he shutteth up a man, and there can be no opening; behold he withholdeth the waters, and they dry up; he sendeth them out, and they overturn the earth, with him is strength and wisdom; and the deceived and the deceiver are his, he leadeth counselors away spoiled, and maketh the judges fools. He looseth the bond of kings, and girdeth there loins with girdle. He leadeth princes away spoiled, and overthroweth the mighty.

When I cry *unto thee*, then shall mine enemies turn back: this I know; for God *is* for me. In God will I praise *his* word; in the LORD will I praise *his* word. In God have I put my trust: I will not be afraid what man can do unto me. Thy vows *are* upon me, O God; I will render praises unto thee. For thou hast delivered my soul from death.

Thus sayeth the Lord, even the captives of the mighty shall be taken away, and the prey of the terrible shall be delivered: for I will contend with him that contendeth with thee, and I will save thy children; and I will feed them that oppress thee with their own flesh; and they shall be drunken with their own blood and all flesh

69

shall know that I the Lord am thy Savior and thy Redeemer, the mighty one of Jacob.

So shout now and let the high praises of God be in our mouth and a two edged sword in our hand, to bind there kings with chains, and there nobles with fetters of irons to execute upon them the judgment written: this honor has all his saints. Praise the Lord for his mercy endureth forever.

I will not be afraid of ten thousands of people that have set themselves against me round about. Arise, O LORD; save me, O my God: for thou hast smitten all mine enemies upon the cheek bone; thou hast broken the teeth of the ungodly. Salvation belongeth unto the LORD; thy blessing is upon thy people. Selah.

And I will come near to you to judgment; and I will be a swift witness against the sorcerers, and against the adulterers, and against false swearers, and against those that oppress the hireling in his wages, the widow, and the fatherless, and that turn aside the stranger from his right, and fear not me, sayeth the LORD of hosts.

For I am the LORD, I change not; therefore ye sons of Jacob are not consumed. God, we bless you and praise in the name of Jesus Christ. Amen.

Warfare Prayer against the Power of the Grave

Father God in the name of Jesus Christ we release with vengeance the blood of the lamb like a tsunami tidal wave against every person, every necromancer, every power, and every spirit from the grave in the name of Jesus Christ.

We bind the Blood of Jesus Christ around every curse, incantation, hex, vex and chant planted from the grave into the heavens around our star, we wrap up everything that has been planted from the grave through necromancy into the heavens and snatch it out of the atmosphere according to 2Cor 10:4; God remove and destroy all seen and unseen curses, that was been planted in the heavens in a bag according to Job 14:17, Jer 49:27.

For the wicked is reserved to the day of destruction? They shall be brought forth to the day of wrath. Who shall declare his way to his face? And who shall repay him for what he hath done? Yet shall he be brought to the grave, and shall remain in the tomb.

God every spirit of every dead relative that is walking the earth realm in the spirit, in our dreams and facilitating wickedness, sickness, stagnation, backwardness, and poverty in our lives and the lives of our family and children; let every spirit be sealed in the tomb in the name of Jesus Christ according to Job 21:32.

God we repent and ask you forgiveness so that you can close and seal up every door way of these familiar spirits that have gained access to our lives to alter our destiny in the name of Jesus Christ according to Rev. 3:7.

God send your fire and the axe of God to destroy every barricade formed by ancestral spirits and evil angels in the heavens that are blocking the release of my blessings in the name of Jesus Christ.

God cut off and break every yoke, every wicked power and spirit from the grave according to Nahum 1:12-15.

In the name of Jesus Christ, depart from me, all ye workers of iniquity; for the LORD hath heard the voice of my weeping. The LORD hath heard my supplication; the LORD will receive my prayer. Let all mine enemies be ashamed and sore vexed: let them return and be ashamed suddenly.

God bring up my soul and the foundation of my life from the grave of every grave robber, and ancestral debt collector in the name Jesus Christ according to Psalm 30:3.

In the name of Jesus Christ, every power troubling my star and my foundation of life from the grave, we curse your powers and your success in the name of Jesus Christ; and every voice from my ancestors releasing instructions for torment and hindrance in my life and my family's life: let your tongue cleave to the roof of your mouth, let your instructions be misunderstood, and let the success of your works be cursed and dried up from the roots according to Mark 11:14, 20, Gen 19:11.

God, send the blood of Yeshua Hamashiah like a tidal wave to locate and destroy every ritual made against my life, summoning spirits from the dead in the name of Jesus Christ.

God destroy with fire every amulet that is used for summoning and controlling every ancestral debt collector from the grave in the name of Jesus Christ.

God send your warrior angels to locate and lock up in fetters and everlasting chains every spirit summoned from the dead of every dead witch, warlock, necromancer, shaman, voodoo and satanic high priest. God seal them in their tomb and have them carried to Tartartus in the name of Jesus Christ of Nazareth according to 2Pet. 2:4, Matt 13:41-42, Job 7:9.

God send your warrior angels to hunt down and bind up every evil angel that is working with every ancestral spirit from the dead in everlasting chains according to Jude 1:6.

God send your salt from the third heaven to locate, cover, bury, and disintegrate every barricade formed by oaths, covenants and curses planted in the heavens and in the earth against my life from every grave and the grave of my ancestors in the name of Jesus Christ.

But I trusted in thee, O LORD: I said, Thou art my God. My times are in thy hand; deliver me from the hand of mine enemies, and from them that persecute me.

Make thy face to shine upon thy servant: save me for thy mercies' sake. Let me not be ashamed, O LORD; for I have called upon thee: let the wicked be ashamed, and let them be silent in the grave.

Let the lying lips be put to silence; which speak grievous things proudly and contemptuously against the righteous in the name of Jesus Christ.

God all those that made terror in the land of the living and have gone down to the nether parts of the pit, let them stay buried in there shame in the blood of Jesus Christ according to Ezek 32:24, 27.

God send your axe and destroy every soul tie, oath, covenant, and contract with every dead relative that operated in the works of witchcraft on both sides of the family going back 70 generations in the name of Jesus Christ.

God we release the blood of Jesus Christ hunt down, locate and we bind in everlasting chains every ancestral debt collector from the grave, going back 70 generations on both side of the family in the name of Jesus Christ according to Jude 1:6.

God don't let my sins and the sins of my fathers consume me to the grave in the name of Jesus Christ according to Job 24:19, Lev. 26:40-42.

For I will ransom them from the power of the grave; I will redeem them from death; O death, I will be thy plagues; O grave, I will be thy destruction; and repentance shall be hid from mine eyes.

God I thank you for redeeming my soul from every power of the grave in the name of Jesus Christ. Oh!! LORD of hosts, God of Israel, that dwellest between the cherubims, thou art the God, even thou alone, of all the kingdoms of the earth; thou hast made heaven and earth. Incline thine ear, O LORD, and hear; open thine eyes, O LORD, and see; and hear all the words that have been spoken from the dead.

Oh God make null and void every command and instruction made from the grave in the name of Yeshua Hamashiah.

We cancel every victory and every sting from the grave in the name of Jesus Christ according to 1Cor. 15: 54-58.

God send fire from the 3rd heaven to burn and destroy every ancestral barricade formed over our star and destiny in the second heaven in the name of Jesus Christ according to Gen. 19:24, 27.

God, as Moses stood between the living and the dead, God, send your warrior angels to stand guard with everlasting chains between the living and the dead to block their passage way from the underworld in the name of the Lord Jesus Christ.

God send your warrior angels to do battle and to lock up in everlasting chains every ancestral spirit and evil angel that has come to steal, kill, and destroy in the name of Jesus Christ.

For as the cloud is consumed and vanisheth away: so is he that goeth down to the grave, shall come up no more. For he shall return no more to his house; neither shall his place know him any more, in the name of Jesus Christ. God, we praise you, and we thank you for the manifestation of this prayer in the name of Jesus Christ. Amen.

Warfare prayer against mind control

Father God in the name of the Lord Jesus Christ we come against all mind control on every level, order, and rank in the name of Jesus Christ; We bind up in everlasting chains the spirit of Haman, that mind manipulating spirit that orchestrates death, destruction, and destitution in the name of Jesus Christ; We destroy with fire all mind binding and mind blinding works in the spirit through psychic meditation via soul ties in the name of Jesus Christ. God we ask that you lift up a standard to stop and block all sensory perception from all satanic forces that bring headaches and tries to bind and blind our minds in the name of Jesus Christ. We break and release our selves and return these illegal transference of demonic thoughts back to the sender according to Plsm 109:17-19.Plsm 18:17.

God we break and release ourselves and lock up there demonic brain waves within themselves in the name of Jesus Christ; Oh God let the headaches be magnified 100 fold upon there own lives in the name of Jesus Christ. God we release the Blood of Jesus Christ to curse the success of all mind manipulation through astral projection and remote viewing in the name of Jesus Christ.

God we call down fire from heaven to destroy every frequency in the blue ether, and we cut every silver cord that they use to teleport their thoughts and intentions in the name of Jesus Christ. Lord we bind up the spirit of scanners that would try to discern and scan our brain waves in the spirit to anticipate our thoughts and moves the name of Jesus Christ according to 2King 6:18.

 Thus saith the Lord GOD; It shall also come to pass, that at the same time shall things come into thy mind, and thou shalt think an evil thought: And I will call for a sword against him throughout all my mountains, saith the Lord GOD: every man's sword shall be against his brother. And I will plead against him with pestilence and with blood; and I will rain upon him, and upon his bands, and upon the many people that are with him, an overflowing rain, and great hailstones, fire, and brimstone. In the name of Jesus Christ according to Ezek 38:10, 21-22, Pslm 18:14.

God let this be the portion to everyone that would work this form of psychic witchcraft, let a spirit of Alzheimer's, backwardness, retardation, and dementia enter into their own mind every time they do this, let it be sealed with in the hemispheres of their own mind in the name of Jesus Christ according to Pslm 18:14.

God let it magnify itself into excruciating pain in the name of Jesus Christ. God we take the sword of The Lord Jesus Christ and chop up the head of every leviathan spirit associated with them as a spirit guide and a spirit help in the name of Jesus Christ.

We curse the success of all divination and prophetic witchcraft through mind control in the name of Jesus Christ. They have seen vanity and lying divination, saying, The LORD saith: and the LORD hath not sent them: and they have made others to hope that they would confirm the word. Therefore thus saith the Lord GOD; Because ye have spoken vanity, and seen lies, therefore, behold, I am against you, saith the Lord GOD.

 And mine hand shall be upon the prophets that see vanity, and that divine lies: they shall not be in the assembly of my people; neither shall they be written in the writing of the house of Israel, neither shall they enter into the land of Israel; nor ye shall know that I am the Lord GOD.

 Now God let your wrath, indignation, judgment be sealed in the bowels of the workers of every level , form, and rank of these types of iniquity until they repent or until YOU fulfill the intents of your heart and judgment according to Jer 30:23-24 , Pslm 7:14-16 ,Plsm 109:17-19 in the name of Jesus Christ amen

Destroying Satan's Voice, The Children of Belial

Father in the name of Jesus Christ, we ask that you destroy the voice of satan, that roaring lion. God, we ask that you destroy his vocal cords and the vocal chords of those that he uses in the earth realm in the name of Jesus Christ. God, confuse their language so that they cannot communicate with one another; confuse the language that they use as a source of communication in the name of Jesus Christ according to Judges 7:20-22.

Lord, let his own sword be the weapon that destroys his voice, and the voice of Belial and his workers of iniquity according to Psalm 37: 14-15. For you said the wicked have drawn out the sword, and have bent their bow, to cast down the poor and needy, and to slay such as be of upright conversation.

Their sword shall enter into their own heart, and their bows shall be broken. Lord God, we thank you for the demonstration of your power. Let every voice uttering incantations and curses, let their throat become dry and their tongue cleave to the roof of their mouth in the name of Jesus Christ.

We shut up the voice of every ancestral debt collector from the grave, we release the judgment of the lake of fire to destroy every work released in the atmosphere, in the heavens, and command fire and brimstone to reign destruction from the throne room of God over every plot, plan, and information released from the grave in the name of the Lord Jesus Christ.

We release the power of Calvary to destroy the power of the Grave in the name of Jesus Christ according to Jer 51:58.

For you said: that the transgressors shall be destroyed together; the end of the wicked shall be cut off. Lord, we thank you for cutting off the wicked in the name of Jesus Christ according to Isaiah 37:6-7.

For you said be not afraid of the words that thou hast heard, wherewith the servants of the king of Assyria have blasphemed me.

Behold, I will send a blast upon him, and he shall hear a rumor, and return to his own land; and I will cause him to fall by the sword in his own land. Let their way be dark and slippery and the angel of the Lord shall chase them, let their way be dark and slippery and the angel of the Lord shall persecute them, for this cause was the Son of Man manifested to destroy the works of the devil!!!!

God, we ask that you lock up the works of their hands according to Psalm 149:8. For you said you will bind their kings in chains and there nobles with fetters of irons. Bind them up and snatch every work of iniquity out of the atmosphere in the name of Jesus Christ according to 2Cor 10:4.

God, cut them off from their power source and spirit helps according to Num 14:9. God, destroy with fire every cage, locker and storage bins that is holding the blessing of wealth and good health and salvation hostage, and let these things be returned 7-fold; for you said if the thief be found, he shall restore sevenfold; he shall give all the substance of his house according to Pro 6:31. God, we destroy every voice that would curse our blessings in the name of Jesus Christ.

God destroy the voice of every ventriloquist that is sending false information into my spiritual hearing in the name of Jesus Christ. God, we break and release our blessings in the name of Jesus Christ.

But the sons of Belial shall be all of them as thorns thrust away, because they cannot be taken with hands. But the man that shall touch them must be fenced with iron and the staff of a spear; and they shall be utterly burned with fire in the same place.

God we curse the power, authority and success of the craftiness of the children of Belial and all ventriloquist, we release confusion and error in their prophetic site, we expose their gift of manipulation in recruiting weak people and hurt people in the name of Jesus Christ. Let every person releasing satanic utterances reap their own calamity according to Proverb 6:15.

And God, we praise you for the manifestation of this prayer and we thank you for releasing your angels according to Psalm 103:20, Matt. 13:41-42, Psalm 68:17, to respond to your word, in the name of Jesus Christ. Amen.

Prayer to Destroy Satanic Pentagrams

Father God in the name of Jesus Christ, according to Isaiah 5:18-24, Matt. 13:41-42, we ask that the mighty hands of Alpha and Omega would gather up, and rip up, destroy, and annihilate all the works, and the symbols of every wiccan, neopagan, and satanic pentagram that has been placed over our health, finances, family, business, ministry, and destiny in the name of Yeshua Hamashiah, according to Jeremiah 51:24-26.

We ask that you bind up the principalities in the hands of Alpha and Omega, that's over every pentagram, black magic, the evil eye, third eye, all seeing eye, that has been sent to destroy us, and snatch them out of the atmosphere and thrown in the lake of Fire in the name of Jesus Christ according to Jude 1:6, 2 pet 2:4, Rev. 20:10.

But thus shall ye deal with them; ye shall destroy their altars, and break down their images, and cut down their groves, and burn their graven images with fire.

Father in the name of Jesus Christ, draw your sword and consume every demonic force released through these works according to Jer. 49:37-38. We bind up, and spoil the goods of every satanic works released according to Job 14:17, and every associated demon according to Luke 11:20-22, 2Pet. 2:4,

God, bring fear and destruction speedily according to Jer. 48: 42-45, and in the name of Yeshua Hamashiah.

Keep me as the apple of the eye; hide me under the shadow of thy wings, from the wicked that oppress me, from my deadly enemies, who compass me about.

They are inclosed in their own fat: with their mouth they speak proudly. They have now compassed us in our steps: they have set their eyes bowing down to the earth.

Like as a lion that is greedy of his prey, and as it were a young lion lurking in secret places. Arise, O LORD, disappoint him, and cast him down; deliver my soul from the wicked, which is thy sword.

We curse the power, the works and the success of every pentagram of every sort , level ,order and rank according to Isaiah 14:10, Psalm 75:10a, Isaiah 5:18-24, Mark 11:14,20.

God, we ask that you send an everlasting fire according to Acts19:19; Amos 2:2-3 to eternally destroy these works, and Lord, we give you the praise for accelerated destruction and complete eternal annihilation according to Jer. 1:11, Gen 19:24,27, Rev 20:10.

And the earth opened her mouth, and swallowed them up together with Korah, when that company died, what time the fire devoured two hundred and fifty men: and they became a sign.

Now God, we choose to thank you and praise you for the out pouring and the anointing of invincibility according to Judges 15:14-15, Psalm 75:10b and the total restoration and release of every prophecy, and every promise of wealth, good health, marital happiness, salvation for our family members, and a long life in its full abundance; for you said that YOU will do exceedingly and abundantly above all we can ask or think.

God, we thank you for the shift and the change according to Gen 39:2 and the manifestation of Faith that is pleasing in you site in the name of Yeshua Hamashiah

But I have trusted in thy mercy; my heart shall rejoice in thy salvation. I will sing unto the LORD, because he hath dealt bountifully with me.

God, we glorify you for the finished works of the cross in the name of Jesus Christ. Amen.

Warfare Prayer against Satanic Devices

Father God in the name of Jesus Christ, God, we repent from everything and every thought that is sin and we confess them in the name of Jesus Christ.

God, we no longer want to be ignorant of satan's devices; we ask that you give us the discernment so that we can discern between the righteous and the wicked, between him that serveth God, and him that serveth him not in the name of Jesus Christ according to Mal 3:18.

God, we praise you, for you disappointeth the devices of the crafty, so that their hands cannot perform their enterprise. He taketh the wise in their own craftiness: and the counsel of the forward is carried headlong.

Why standest thou afar off, O LORD? Why hidest thou thyself in times of trouble? The wicked in his pride doth persecute the poor: let them be taken in the devices that they have imagined in the name of the Lord Jesus Christ.

God, let those that have devised devices through meditations, spoken word curses to be taken in what they have imagined in the name of Jesus Christ according to Psalm 10: 1-2.

God!!! Break thou the arm of the wicked and the evil man: seek out his wickedness till thou findest none in the name of Jesus Christ. How oft the candle of the wicked is put out! And how oft cometh their destruction upon them! God, distributeth sorrows in his anger. They are as stubble before the wind and as chaff that the storm carrieth away.

God layeth up his iniquity for his children: he rewardeth him, and he shall know it. His eyes shall see his destruction, and he shall drink of the wrath of the Almighty.

God, we thank you for putting out their candle and for the wrath that you are releasing upon them in the name of Jesus Christ; God, seal your wrath in their bowels in the name of Jesus Christ according to Psalm 109:17-19.

A good man obtaineth favor of the LORD; but a man (and woman) of wicked devices will he condemn. A man shall not be established by wickedness; but the root of the righteous shall not be moved.

God, we condemn every device spoken out of their mouth, their plans, and their counsels; and we curse and condemn their establishment in the name of Jesus Christ according to Prv 12:2-3.

God destroy all of their devices that proceedeth out of their mouth in the name of Jesus Christ.

For by the word of the LORD were the heavens made; and all the host of them by the breath of his mouth. He gathereth the waters of the sea together as an heap; he layeth up the depth in storehouses.

Let all the earth fear the LORD; let all the inhabitants of the world stand in awe of him. For he spake, and it was done; he commanded, and it stood fast. The LORD bringeth the counsel of the heathen to naught; he maketh the devices of the people of none effect.

Rest in the LORD, and wait patiently for him: fret not thyself because of him who prospereth in his way, because of the man who bringeth wicked devices to pass.

Cease from anger, and forsake wrath; fret not thyself in any wise to do evil. For evildoers shall be cut off; but those that wait upon the LORD, they shall inherit the earth.

God we praise you as you cut off the evil doers. Oh God, we magnify your name as you return all the devices of the wicked to the sender and seal it in their bowels in the name of Jesus Christ according to Psalm 109:17-19.

But the LORD is with me as a mighty terrible one: therefore my persecutors shall stumble, and they shall not prevail; they shall be greatly ashamed, for they shall not prosper; their everlasting confusion shall never be forgotten.

But, O LORD of hosts, that tryest the righteous, and seest the reins and the heart, let me see thy vengeance on them; for unto thee have I opened my cause.

Sing unto the LORD, praise ye the LORD: for he hath delivered the soul of the poor from the hand of evildoers.

All Mighty God, we thank you for the manifestation of the words of this prayer; and God, we thank you for the performance that is going to wrought by your hands; and Lord God, we give you the praise in the name of Jesus Christ. Amen.

Prayers to Remove Marks that attract Demonic Attacks

Father God in the name of Jesus Christ, we confess our sins and the sins of our fathers, for you said: If they shall confess their iniquity, and the iniquity of their fathers, with their trespass which they trespassed against me, and that also they have walked contrary unto me. And *that* I also have walked contrary unto them, and have brought them into the land of their enemies; if then their uncircumcised hearts be humbled, and they then accept of the punishment of their iniquity. Then will I remember my covenant with Jacob, and also my covenant with Isaac, and also my covenant with Abraham will I remember; and I will remember the land.

Father God in the name of Jesus Christ, we ask that you would forgive and take the blood of Jesus Christ to erase and remove every mark, every miphga that is caused by my sins and the iniquity of our fathers in the name of Jesus Christ.

God, we ask that you remove every mark that acts as a beacon to make us an object of attack in the name of Jesus Christ according to Job 7:20.

God we ask that you would erase every mark, every miphga, with the blood of Jesus Christ that was caused by ungodly oaths, pledges, and agreements to demons, organizations, and witchcraft powers and sorcery, made by ourselves and our ancestors in the name of the Lord Jesus Christ.

God we ask the you erase, burn and destroy every mark, every miphga placed upon our life and blood line caused by family dedications made to satan going back 70 generations And going forward 3 to 4 generations on both sides of the family in the name of Jesus Christ.

God, we destroy by fire and erase by the blood of the lamb every hand writing and ordinance made through witchcraft and charismatic witchcraft that has marked us for open attacks from others that operate in the occult powers in the name of Jesus Christ.

Thus sayeth the LORD, thy redeemer, and he that formed thee from the womb: I *am* the LORD that maketh all *things*; that stretcheth forth the heavens alone; that spreadeth abroad the earth by myself; that frustrateth the tokens of the liars, and maketh diviners mad; that turneth wise *men* backward, and maketh their knowledge foolish.

God take the blood of Jesus Christ and remove and erase from existence every evil mark that was planted in my dreams in the name of Jesus Christ.

God erase every mark of financial lack and misfortunes from my life with the blood of Jesus Christ, in the name of Jesus Christ.

God erase every anti-marriage, unsuccessful marriage, and relationship mark from my life with the blood of Jesus Christ, in the name of Jesus Christ.

We close every door way for any new marks of evil attacks to be placed on our life at the point of entry in the name of Jesus Christ according to Rev 3:7.

We destroy by fire from the throne room of God every mark that was placed on our star in the heavens through astral projection in the name of Jesus Christ according to 2Kings 23:15.

God destroy by fire every satanic and astral altar that acts as a beacon to place curses on our lives in the name of Jesus Christ according to 1Kings 13:5.

God destroy by fire every mark that would attract sickness in the name of Jesus Christ.

God destroy and erase with the blood of Jesus Christ every mark that acts as a beacon that would attract poverty and failure in my life in the name of Jesus Christ.

In the name of Jesus Christ, God, destroy by fire every mark the enemy uses to locate me in the spirit and where I rest in the name of Jesus Christ according to Ruth 3:4.

Deliver me from mine enemies, O my God; defend me from them that rise up against me. Deliver me from the workers of iniquity, and save me from bloody men.

God we ask that you remove with the blood of Jesus Christ every mark that would attract the enemies' arrows to every area of my life in the name of Jesus Christ.

Every day they wrest my words: all their thoughts *are* against me for evil. They gather themselves together, they hide themselves, and they mark my steps, when they wait for my soul. Shall they escape by iniquity? In *thine* anger cast down the people, O God.

Lord purge us with hyssop so we can be clean; wash us so we can be whiter than snow. God purge us of every mark that the enemy has planted on our life and our family and children in the name of Jesus Christ according to Psalm 51:7, Num 31:23.

When I cry *unto thee*, then shall mine enemies turn back: this I know; for God *is* for me. In God will I praise *his* word: in the LORD will I praise *his* word. In God have I put my trust: I will not be afraid what man can do unto me.

Thy vows *are* upon me, O God; I will render praises unto thee. For thou hast delivered my soul from death: *wilt* not *thou deliver* my feet from falling, that I may walk before God in the light of the living? God, we thank you and praise you for there is nothing too hard for you and we give you the glory.

We bind in everlasting chains every spirit of Absalom that would release kill orders and mark us for death, failure and destitution in the name of Jesus Christ.

God we thank you for the removal of all evil marks that have aided the enemy for attacks against our life and God we give you the glory and we give you the praise.

God we return every mark to the sender in the name of Jesus Christ according to Psalm 109:17-19.

Now Lord, hide us in the secret place under the shadow of your wings in the name of Jesus Christ according to Psalm 91:4.

God cover us and bind us in the blood of Jesus Christ so that not another mark can be placed or planted on us in the heavens and in the earth in the name of Jesus Christ.

From henceforth, let no man trouble me; for I bear in my body the marks of the Lord Jesus.

God we ask that we receive the marks of the Lord Jesus, to receive the blessings of the Lord Jesus Christ, favor that will compass us like a shield, protection from the terror by day and the arrows by night, and unhindered, unexpected, miracles in the name of Jesus Christ according to Gen 4:24, Psalm 5:12.

Mark the perfect *man*, and behold the upright: for the end of *that* man *is* peace. But the transgressors shall be destroyed together: the end of the wicked shall be cut off.

But the salvation of the righteous *is* of the LORD; *he is* their strength in the time of trouble. And the LORD shall help them, and deliver them; he shall deliver them from the wicked, and save them, because they trust in him.

But verily God hath heard *me*; he hath attended to the voice of my prayer.

Blessed *be* God, which hath not turned away my prayer, nor his mercy from me.

Brethren, the grace of our Lord Jesus Christ *be* with your spirit. Amen.

Warfare Prayer Against
Invisible Walls, Barriers, and Barricades

Father God in the name of Yeshua Hamashiah, we ask that you rip up and destroy every invisible barrier that is over our family, health, finances, salvation and ministry, barriers that are constructed and enforced through spoken word curses, Blood line Curses, iron like curses, witchcraft prayers, necromancy, amulets, candle burning, hoodoo, voodoo, charismatic witchcraft, Jezebelic witchcraft, homemade witchcraft, hexes, vexes, envy, jealousy, evil eye stares, astral projections, enchantments, demonic hand writings and ordinances, group psychic meditations, and ungodly soul ties to the living and the dead, evil angels, dark angels, ancestral spirits in the name of Jesus Christ, according to Acts 19:19, Job 14:17, 2 Cor 10:4-5, Matt. 13:41-42, Job 4:8-9.

We bind in everlasting chains every wicked spirit, every dark angel, every evil angel, every familiar spirit, every ancestral spirit, every unclean spirit, every python spirit, every spirit wife, every spirit husband, every imp, every demon, every power from the grave that forms these barriers, watches these gates, enforces these walls, binds these yokes, and every smith that forms these weapons; we cast you out of your position of power and authority with the finger of God in the name of Jesus Christ according to Matt 13:41-42, 2Pet. 2:4, Exodus 8:19, Mark 3:27, Luke 11:20, Isaiah 54:17.

In the name of Jesus Christ, no weapon that is formed against thee shall prosper.

Hear me when I call, O God of my righteousness: thou hast enlarged me when I was in distress; have mercy upon me, and hear my prayer.

God destroy with vengeances every known and unknown invisible wall and barrier that is a hindrance to our lives, prosperity, business and ministry. God, rip it up from top to bottom, every thing that is stagnating our goals, our dreams, our destiny, our hidden potentials, and the will of God for our lives in the name of Jesus Christ according to Jer. 50:15, Psalm 68:17, Jer 30:22-24.

God destroy every yoke, for you said that you shall loose the bands of wickedness and the yokes shall be destroyed because of the anointing according to Isaiah 10:27.

The LORD tryeth the righteous; but the wicked and him that loveth violence his soul hateth. Upon the wicked he shall rain snares, fire and brimstone, and a horrible tempest; this shall be the portion of their cup.

God we ask that you destroy every obstacle, and every Jericho wall that is in our lives, walls summoned by satanic forces that are constructed to block the release of our blessings, and set time of favor in the name of Jesus Christ according to Josh 6:20, Isaiah 25:11-12.

Lord we lift up our voice like a shofar as did your priests and the children of Israel, in the name of Jesus Christ according to Heb 11:30.

God we thank you, for giving us this testimony that gates of hell shall not prevail. God, release the faith, the power, and the anointing from on high, that is needed to prevail against the gates of hell, gates of sickness, gates of poverty, gates of oppression, gates of depression, gates of lethargy, gates of wandering, gates of confusion, gates of the grave. God, destroy every gate of hell that is known and unknown in the name of Jesus Christ according to Matt 16:18, Duet. 1:30, Jer 51:58.

God send thee anointing, the spirit of might, as you anointed Samson to uproot the gates of Gaza, anoint us Lord God to uproot these gates in our lives in the name of Jesus Christ according to Judges 16:3; 2Chr. 26:5-6.

We release divine judgment and destruction against every barrier of impossibility attached to my life through witchcraft and ancestral covenants in the name of Yeshua Hamashiah.

We command fire to come down from the throne room of God, to burn, destroy, desolate, throw down, and annihilate every wall, every barrier that acts as a fortress and a blockade over the release of our blessings, and our breakthroughs in the name of Jesus Christ according Amos 2:2-3; Gen 19:24, 27.

For thus sayeth the LORD of hosts; the broad walls of Babylon shall be utterly broken, and her high gates shall be burned with fire; and the people shall labor in vain, and the folk in the fire, and they shall be weary. God, destroy every high gate and barrier that is set up against our mental, physical, and financial breakthroughs in the name of Jesus Christ according to Jer 51:58.

God, send your warrior angels to breakthrough every barrier as did David's 3 mighty men in the name of Jesus Christ according to 2Sam 23:16.

God, send Michael and Your end time warrior angels to annihilate every 3-fold cord barrier, every stumbling block, every booby-trap, and every trap that repeats cycles, caused by the sign of the times and seasons in the name of Jesus Christ according to Rev 12:7-9, Psalm 68:17.

In the name Jesus Christ, set engines of war against their walls, and with axes he will break down there towers!!

God destroy every snare: every snare of the fowler; snares of poverty, snares of backwardness, snares of stagnation, snares of procrastination, snares of sabotage, snares connected to blood line curses, snares from ancestral spirits, snares of mammon, poverty, and fear that form a threefold cord, that are time released to block, hinder and discourage at the point of every breakthrough in our lives in the name of the Lord Jesus Christ.

Snares of being in the right place at the wrong time, snares of being a day late and a dollar short, snares of shame from your past, snares of too little too late, snares of if I would of, could of, should of; God uncover, uproot, dismantle, purge and destroy with fire every known and unknown deep secret snares in our lives, in the name of the Lord Jesus Christ of Nazareth.

God destroy with fire every snare connected to family secrets in the name of Jesus Christ; I will say of the LORD, *He is* my refuge and my fortress: my God; in him will I trust. Surely he shall deliver thee from the snare of the fowler, *and* from the noisome pestilence.

God we ask that you remove every 3-fold cord barrier that has been caused by sin, disobedience, and not tithing consistently. God we repent, and confess our faults, and seek your forgiveness so that we can receive the finances to start giving and tithing consistently in the name of Jesus Christ according to 1 John 1:7, 9.

God, close every door at the point of entry and remove every barrier caused by the sins of our fathers, in the name of Yeshua Hamashiah according to Lev 26:40-42.

For your word says, If they shall confess their iniquity, and the iniquity of their fathers, with their trespass which they trespassed against me, and that also they have walked contrary unto me. And that I also have walked contrary unto them, and have brought them into the land of their enemies; if then their uncircumcised hearts be humbled, and they then accept the punishment of their iniquity:

Then will I remember my covenant with Jacob, and also my covenant with Isaac, and also my covenant with Abraham will I remember; and I will remember the land.

God we repent, and we ask that you break and release us, revive us, restore us, through the same spirit that raised Jesus Christ from the dead to bring us into divine acceleration, and Lord God we bless your Holy name and we praise you, we give you the glory, we give you the honor, we thank you for the grace that was needed to endure in the name of Jesus Christ.

For the wicked in *his* pride doth persecute the poor: let them be taken in the devices that they have imagined.

By the power of the Holy Ghost we release divine judgment and total destruction against every specially designed satanic and witchcraft barrier assigned to our family and our lives since birth in the name of the Lord Jesus Christ.

Oh let the wickedness of the wicked come to an end; but establish the just: for the righteous God tryeth the hearts and reins.

And Jabez called on the God of Israel, saying, Oh that thou wouldest bless me indeed, and enlarge my coast, and that thine hand might be with me, and that thou wouldest keep *me* from evil, that it may not grieve me! And God granted him that which he requested.

God we thank you for the prayer of Jabez that it would release the enlargement of our coast, that would destroy barriers and release your manifold blessings on our life, we praise your Holy name for the manifestation of this prayer in our lives, oh God, in the name of Jesus Christ.

His name shall endure for ever: his name shall be continued as long as the sun; and *men* shall be blessed in him; all nations shall call him blessed.

Blessed *be* the LORD God, the God of Israel, who only doeth wondrous things. And blessed *be* his glorious name for ever: and let the whole earth be filled *with* his glory.

God, we thank you for the manifestation of this prayer in the name of the Lord Jesus Christ. Amen!!

Warfare Prayer against Jezebel

Now Father, we release the anointing of Elijah to prophesy doom against Ahab and Jezebel according to 1Kings 22:19-24; and we release the Anointing of Elisha to instruct the prophets to anoint the end time Jehu's to be relentless and to release a double portion of that anointing to combat against Jezebel and the host in her kingdom according to 2Kings 9:6-10:14.

And it came to pass, that Jehu was executing judgment upon the house of Ahab and Jezebel. God we release your judgment and wrath against every work from this kingdom in the name of Jesus Christ.

We call forth eunuchs to throw her down from her high place to be trodden by horses according 2Kings 9:33; and we release the dogs of Jezreel to eat her flesh works. God, let the dogs out according to 2Kings 9:36-37, in the name of the Lord Jesus Christ.

God send your warrior angels with the sword of Jehu to warfare with vengeance and annihilation against the kingdom of Ahab and Jezebel in the name of Jesus Christ according to 1 kings 19:17.

Lord open up the kennels of heaven and send the dogs of Jezreel to hunt down, locate, and to chew up every Jezebelic prayers, psychic prayers, well meaning prayers that are not God's will for our lives, all mind manipulation, group controlling witchcraft and its works, in our churches, and in our lives.

We break covenant, severe, cut, burn, blow up, undam, and destroy all their works, and break every 3-fold demonic cords with an everlasting fire for our God is a consuming fire in the name of Jesus Christ, according to 2Kings 9:22, Judges 16:9.

Even as I have seen: they that plow iniquity, and sow wickedness, reap the same, by the blast of God they perish, and by the breath of his nostrils are they consumed according to Job 4:8-9.

God, send a blast upon him, and he shall hear a rumor, and return to his own land; and I will cause him to fall by the sword of his own land, according to Isaiah 37:7. God, release this according to your word in the name of Yeshua Hamashiah.

But the LORD is with me as a mighty terrible one: therefore my persecutors shall stumble, and they shall not prevail; they shall be greatly ashamed, for they shall not prosper; their everlasting confusion shall never be forgotten.

But, O LORD of hosts, that tryest the righteous, and seest the reins and the heart, let me see thy vengeance on them: for unto thee have I opened my cause.

Sing unto the LORD, praise ye the LORD: for he hath delivered the soul of the poor from the hand of evildoers.

The heathen are sunk down in the pit *that* they made: in the net which they hid is their own foot taken. For the LORD is known *by* the judgment *which* he executeth: and the wicked is snared in the work of his own hands.

Even as I have seen, they that plow iniquity, and sow wickedness, reap the same. By the blast of God they perish, and by the breath of his nostrils are they consumed. The roaring of the lion, and the voice of the fierce lion, and the teeth of the young lions, are broken. The old lion perisheth for lack of prey, and the stout lion's whelps are scattered abroad.

God we command their spirit guides and spirit helps to be located and locked up in everlasting chains, and their protection and defenses to depart from them in the name of Jesus Christ according to Num 14:9, Psalm 75:10a, Isaiah 14:10, Mic 3:6 a,b,c.

And mine eye shall not spare thee, neither will I have pity; but I will recompense thy ways upon thee, and thine abominations shall be in the midst of thee; and ye shall know that I am the LORD.

And God, we praise you and magnify your Holy name in the name of Yeshua Hamashiah. Amen.

Prayer to Destroy the Black Widows Web

Father God in the name of Jesus Christ, we ask that you send fire to destroy every spiritual cobweb that has been placed over my life and finances by the hand of every black widow in the name of Jesus Christ according to Act 19:19, Jer 51:58.

We destroy with the whirl wind of the Lord and the fierce anger of the Lord, every cobweb, and spider webs, constructed through spoken word curses, chants, thoughts and homemade witchcraft in the name of Jesus Christ according to Jer 30:22-24.

We apply the blood of Jesus Christ to remove satan's mark from off of our life, all marks that attracts poverty, shame, disgrace and sickness. God send your angels to blot it out and erase it from ever existing in the name of the Lord Jesus Christ.

God purge us with hyssop so we can be clean, wash us so we can be whiter than snow. God purges every satanic mark or tattoo that has been placed on us by satanic trackers in the earth realm and in the heavens to target us in the name of Jesus Christ according to Isaiah 44:25.

We call on the hand of God to locate and rip up every contract, plan, drawing, draft, and smash every scale model of our life that is in the hand of every black widow in the name of Jesus Christ according to 2Cor. 10:4, 1Pet. 3:22, Job 37:6-8.

Let his children be continually vagabonds, and beg: let them seek *their bread* also out of their desolate places. Let the extortioner catch all that he hath; and let the strangers spoil his labor. Let there be none to extend mercy unto him in the name of Jesus Christ.

We release the judgment of God to contend against the works of every Black widow operating in our churches in the name of Jesus Christ according to Obadiah 4, Romans 1:28-2:4.

Yea, he sent out his arrows, and scattered them; and he shot out lightning's, and discomfited them.

We curse there power, wisdom, and the success of every satanic assignment against the church in the name of Jesus Christ according to Isaiah 14:10; Isaiah 44:25.

We break and release ourselves from every incantation and conjuration that has been targeted against our success and prosperity. God over turn and return their works and seal it, double seal it, and triple seal it in their very bowels according to Psalm 109:17-19, Psalm 79:12.

Let the intents of their heart be sealed to manifest in their destiny in the name of Jesus Christ; for as they love cursing so let it come upon them, and as they love not blessing, so let it be far from them according to Psalm 109.

Even as I have seen, they that plow iniquity, and sow wickedness, reap the same. By the blast of God they perish, and by the breath of his nostrils are they consumed. The roaring of the lion, and the voice of the fierce lion, and the teeth of the young lions, are broken. The old lion perisheth for lack of prey, and the stout lion's whelps are scattered abroad.

Now is the end come upon thee, and I will send mine anger upon thee, and will judge thee according to thy ways, and will recompense upon thee all thine abominations.

God we release your word and your warrior angels to frustrate every envious witchcraft operation that has been assigned against my life, family, ministry, business, and our forward progress in the name of Jesus Christ according to Matt 13:41-42, Psalm 68:17.

Thus sayeth the LORD, thy redeemer, and he that formed thee from the womb, I am the LORD that maketh all things; that stretcheth forth the heavens alone; that spreadeth abroad the earth by myself; that frustrateth the tokens of the liars, and maketh diviners mad; that turneth wise men backward, and maketh their knowledge foolish.

Let their table become a snare before them: and that which should have been for their welfare, let it become a trap. Let their eyes be darkened, that they see not; and make their loins continually to shake. Pour out thine indignation upon them, and let thy wrathful anger take hold of them. Let their habitation be desolate; and let none dwell in their tents in the name of Jesus Christ according to Psalm 69:22-25.

My lips shall greatly rejoice when I sing unto thee; and my soul, which thou hast redeemed. My tongue also shall talk of thy righteousness all the day long: for they are confounded, for they are brought unto shame that seek my hurt.

But the wicked shall perish, and the enemies of the LORD shall be as the fat of lambs: they shall consume; into smoke shall they consume away.

God we give you the praise, we magnify your name, we glorify your name, we exalt your name, we lift you up for you are the King of Kings, and the Lord of Lords; and we thank you, Jesus, for answered prayer in Jesus Name, Amen.

Prayer of Wisdom Against the Spirit of Absalom

Father God in the name of Jesus Christ, God, we call on your power, the power of the Holy Ghost to open our eyes and ears to point out every person that is operating in the spirit of Absalom in the ministry in the name of Jesus Christ.

Then shall ye return, and discern between the righteous and the wicked, between him that serveth God and him that serveth him not in the name of Jesus Christ according to Mal. 3:18.

God point out every person that is close to us, or that is trying to get close and reveal their secret agenda in exact detail in the name of Jesus Christ.

God we ask that you rip up every cloak and spiritual covering that helps to keep their agenda hidden and secret in the name of Jesus Christ.

God deliver those that mean well, but have allowed the enemy to use them in the name of Jesus Christ according to Isaiah 6:5-7. God, let them see their faults, and confess to them openly, and repent from them in the name of Jesus Christ.

God cause them to fast and pray until they are purged and receive deliverance in the name of Jesus Christ.

God remove those in the ministry that are evil and no good, and that have put on a disguise as a sanctified saint in the name of Jesus Christ according 2Kings 24:3.

For God is not mocked what so ever a man soweth, so shall he reap. God we ask that you take the hand of God to remove every person that is trying to recruit people into witchcraft in the name of Jesus Christ according to 1Pet 3:22, Matt 13:41-42.

He winketh with his eyes, he speaketh with his feet, he teacheth with his fingers; forwardness is in his heart, he deviseth mischief continually; he soweth discord. Therefore shall his calamity come suddenly; suddenly shall he be broken without remedy.

Holy Ghost fires remove the covering, and disguise of every person that enemy has planted to infiltrate the ministry in the name of Jesus Christ.

God, we curse their power, wisdom, success, influence, spirit guides, spirit helps, and their anointing in the name of Jesus Christ according to Isaiah 44:25, Num 14:9.

Now I beseech you, brethren, mark them which cause divisions and offences contrary to the doctrine which ye have learned; and avoid them. For they that are such serve not our Lord Jesus Christ, but their own belly; and by good words and fair speeches deceive the hearts of the simple.

Holy Ghost fire shut down there powers, wisdom and influence that they have in our ministry in the name of Jesus Christ according to Isaiah 44:25.

God, we release backwardness and confusion upon every person operating in the Absalom spirit in the name of Jesus Christ.
God, let every one of them get hung in a tree in the name of Jesus Christ.

We bind up the strong man of recruitment that is anointed to release and sow discord in the ministry in the name of Jesus Christ according to Prv 6:14-15.

Cursed be he that doeth the work of the LORD deceitfully in the name of Jesus Christ.

We curse their wisdom, power, success and campaign efforts in our ministry, and in our church in the name of Jesus Christ according to Psalm 36:11.

God, send your power to break and destroy their ranks of power, position and influence in the name Jesus Christ according to Judges 7:20-22.

Therefore, thou son of man, prepare thee stuff for removing, and remove by day in their sight.

God give us the wisdom and assistance in removing every Absalom that are in key positions in the ministry, in the name of Jesus Christ according to 2Sam. 18:10.

Arise, O LORD; let not man prevail: let the heathen be judged in thy sight. Put them in fear, O LORD.

God we curse the wisdom and success of every person using Jezebelic witchcraft to influence people in key positions in the name of Jesus Christ.

The Son of man shall send forth his angels, and they shall gather out of his kingdom all things that offend, and them which do iniquity.

God we thank you for their deliverance and if necessary, the replacements that are people after your own heart, that are fit for the positions to your approval in the name of Jesus Christ.
God, let those that need to be immediately removed, be removed by your hand, oh God, in a form or fashion that you see fit to remove them in the name of Jesus Christ according to 1Pet 3:22.

God give us the wisdom and courage in handling the removal, demotion, or repositioning of every longtime Absalom, that has kept his identity and agenda secret in the name of Jesus Christ.

God remove from me the blinders that are over my eyes and the hurt that will come upon my heart in the name of Jesus Christ. And now also the axe is laid unto the root of the trees: therefore every tree which bringeth not forth good fruit is hewn down, and cast into the fire.

God send your angels with the axe of God to chop down every tree rooted person that doesn't want to move, that needs to be moved in the name of Jesus Christ according to Matt 3:10.

God we stand in proxy for those who were misled and went astray and ask that they be corrected and that the will of God will overtake there life in the name of Jesus Christ.

God we ask that you purge and remove the spirit of Absalom that is within us that would cause us to be in rebellion to you, oh God. God, we repent and ask for our own personal deliverance in the name of Jesus Christ according to Isaiah 6:5-7.

Forsake me not, O LORD: O my God, be not far from me. Make haste to help me, O Lord my salvation.

Warfare Prayer Against Spoken Word Curses

Father God in the name of Jesus Christ, we repent for the Kingdom of God has Come nigh unto us.

God we forgive those that have brought harm to us, by way of Charismatic witchcraft through psychic prayers, and spoken word curses in the name of Jesus Christ.

God purge my heart, mind, body, spirit and soul of all resentment and unforgiveness against all known and unknown worker's of iniquity in the name of Jesus Christ.

God remove everything that would stop this prayer from being heard and answered in the name of Jesus Christ.

Hold not thy peace, O God of my praise; for the mouth of the wicked and the mouth of the deceitful are opened against me: they have spoken against me with a lying tongue. They compassed me about also with words of hatred; and fought against me without a cause. For my love they are my adversaries: but I *give myself unto* prayer, and they have rewarded me evil for good, and hatred for my love.

God you said, Ask of me, and I shall give *thee* the heathen *for* thine inheritance, and the uttermost parts of the earth *for* thy possession. Thou shalt break them with a rod of iron; thou shalt dash them in pieces like a potter's vessel.

I will not be afraid of ten thousands of people that have set *themselves* against me round about. Arise, O LORD; save me, O my God: for thou hast smitten all mine enemies *upon* the cheek bone; thou hast broken the teeth of the ungodly.

Lead me, O LORD, in thy righteousness because of mine enemies; make thy way straight before my face. For there is no faithfulness in their mouth; their inward part is very wickedness; their throat is an open sepulcher; they flatter with their tongue. Destroy thou them, O God; let them fall by their own counsels; cast them out in the multitude of their transgressions; for they have rebelled against thee.

Oh let the wickedness of the wicked come to an end; but establish the just: for the righteous God tryeth the hearts and reins.

Let mine adversaries be clothed with shame, and let them cover themselves with their own confusion, as with a mantle, let the extortioner catch all that he hath, and let the strangers spoil his labor; let there be none to extend mercy unto him and as he loved cursing, so let it come unto him; and as he delighteth not in blessing, so let it be far from him, as he clothed himself with cursing like a garment, so let it come into his own bowels like water, and like oil into his bones.

The LORD tryeth the righteous: but the wicked and him that loveth violence his soul hateth. Upon the wicked he shall rain snares, fire and brimstone, and an horrible tempest: this shall be the portion of their cup.

God let the words of this prayer hunt down and locate every person, every Balaam that was hired to curse us, every group and confederacy, and manifest itself to the fullest extent in their lives in the name of Jesus Christ.

Let the words of this prayer be the portion of their cup in the name of Jesus Christ.

When he shall be judged, let him be condemned: and let his prayer become sin. Let his days be few in the name of Jesus Christ.

The wicked have drawn out the sword, and have bent their bow, to cast down the poor and needy, and to slay such as be of upright conversation. Their sword shall enter into their own heart, and their bows shall be broken.

God we ask that you take the hand of God, according to 1Pet 3:22, and break and release us from every spoken word curses, Jezebelic curses, psychic prayers and meditations in the name of Jesus Christ.

God bind up all words of hurt and shame released by our parents and love ones that are stored in our memory banks from birth in the name of Jesus Christ.

Bind up every spirit of wickedness that has attached itself, to these words of hurt and shame in the name of Jesus Christ.

We take the hand of God to gather all of them up and put them in a bag according to Job 14:17, and rip it out of the atmosphere, oh God, we rip them out of the second heaven, and out of our heart, mind and soul in the name of Jesus Christ.

We bind up in everlasting Chains every spirit, every evil angel, every dark angel, every unclean spirit, and all things that bring offence that were released against us in the name of Jesus Christ according to Matt 13;41-42, 2Pet 2:4.

We curse the wisdom, timing, and success of every curse that was spoken by every person over our life since birth in the name of Jesus Christ.

We release the wrath of God with fire and hailstones to locate, destroy, overthrow, and over turn every utterance and thought from the children of Belial in the name of Jesus Christ.

Let his posterity be cut off; *and* in the generation following let their name be blotted out. Let the iniquity of his fathers be remembered with the LORD; and let not the sin of his mother be blotted out.

Let them be before the LORD continually that he may cut off the memory of them from the earth. Because that he remembered not to shew mercy, but persecuted the poor and needy man, that he might even slay the broken in heart.

Let this *be* the reward of mine adversaries from the LORD, and of them that speak evil against my soul.

Help me, O LORD my God: O save me according to thy mercy: That they may know that this is thy hand; that thou, LORD, hast done it. Let them curse, but bless thou: when they arise, let them be ashamed; but let thy servant rejoice.

I will greatly praise the LORD with my mouth; yea, I will praise him among the multitude. For he shall stand at the right hand of the poor, to save him from those that condemn his soul. And God, we give you the Praise in the mighty name of Yeshua Hamashiah. Amen.

Warfare Prayer Against Charismatic Witchcraft

Father God in the name of Jesus Christ, we come before your throne repenting and asking for forgiveness, oh God, of our sins and iniquities and the iniquities of our fathers in the name of Jesus Christ.

We pray and ask that you remove all bitterness and resentment that is in our heart against all known and unknown parties and individuals that have been operating in charismatic witchcraft against my life, ministry, family, education, business, finances and set time of breakthroughs in the name of Jesus Christ.

God we thank you for it is written that the wickedness of the wicked has come to an end in the name of Yeshua Hamashiah according to Psalm 7:9.

God let those that have devised devices through meditations, spoken word curses be overtaken and consumed in what they have imagined in their minds and in their hearts against me in the name of Jesus Christ according to Psalm 10: 1-2.

God we release confusion, turmoil, backwardness, stagnation, and spiritual epilepsy in the prophetic gift, discernment and revelation of every person that would use there gifts and the gifts of others to receive plans and strategies to launch an attack against our lives, business, ministry, health, and finances in the name of Jesus Christ according to Isaiah 44:25, Gen 19:11, Psalm 35:26.

God let every psychic and Jezebelic prayer prayed against us become sin to your ears and counted as judgment against those that have prayed them in the name of Jesus Christ.

God break and release us from these prayers and meditations, overturn and return them and seal it in the bowels of the senders in the name of Jesus Christ according to Psalm 109:17-19.

Let those that have marked us for an open bounty without cause, receive the manifestation of the wrath and fury of almighty God in their own lives in the name of Jesus Christ according to Jer 30:22-24.

Let God arise and bring the plans of my oppressors to nothing in the name of Jesus Christ according to Psalm 7:9, Psalm 35:4.

Oh God, arise and let my oppressors be bound with a blitzkrieg of torment, turmoil, panic, havoc, destruction, and paranoia, let it be sealed in the minds and the bowels of every person that is seeking after my soul in the name of Jesus Christ according to Psalm 79:12, Psalm 7:15-16.

But as for them whose heart walketh after the heart of their detestable things and their abominations, I will recompense their way upon their own heads, saith the Lord GOD.

Let all those that consult darkness to oppress me, let them receive the manifestation of the works of their own hands in the name of Jesus Christ according to Isaiah 19:14-16, Psalm 109.

God, send your warrior angels to hunt down, locate, and lock up in everlasting chains their spirit guides, spirit helps, protection, spies and attendants in the name of Jesus Christ according to 2Pet 2:4.

God, by the power of the Holy Ghost we release civil war in every Jezebelic group that has organized to targeted us for attacks in the name of Jesus Christ according to Judges 7:20-22, Psalm 37:14-15.

God let them battle one against the other until they annihilate one another with their own hatred, prayers and fastings in the name of Jesus Christ.

Let every weapon of psychic prayer and meditation backfire and blow up in the face of the senders in the name of Jesus Christ.

God paralyze every demon, every wicked ancestral spirit, every evil angel, dark angel, blood line strong man that has attached itself to any thoughts, chants, prayers, and meditations of every jezebel, belial, black widow and minister of satan in the name of Yeshua Hamashiah.

Oh God, deliver my soul from the snares of the wicked in the name of Yeshua Hamashiah.

God be an adversary to my strong adversaries in the name of Jesus Christ.

Let their way be dark and slippery and let the angel of the Lord chase them.

Let their way be dark and slippery and let the angel of the Lord persecute them.

God let not mine enemies rejoice over me in the name of the Lord Jesus Christ.

God we curse the operation and the success of all charismatic witchcraft and the power of the dog that is operating in our church in the name of Jesus Christ according to Mark 11:14, 20.

The LORD executeth righteousness and judgments for all that are oppressed. He made known his ways unto Moses, his acts unto the children of Israel. How many are the days of thy servant? When wilt thou execute judgment on them that persecute me?

For God shall bring every work into judgment, with every secret thing, whether it be good, or whether it be evil.

God we release the persecuting fire of the Holy Ghost and blast from the breath of your nostrils to either bring them into true repentance or to permanently remove them from our churches and our place of worship, every minister of satan in the name of the Lord Jesus Christ according to Job 4:8-9, Job 20:5-15.

God send the fire of the Holy Ghost to convict, bring fear, and up root those that have infiltrated and entrenched themselves in the ministry and prayer groups, that you know oh God, that has no intention of repenting. God let them drink from the cup of your wrath until they are consumed in their own wickedness in the name of Jesus Christ according to Est. 9:24-25.

God, we release civil war in the hearts and the minds of those that would try to reorganize, regenerate, restructure their operation of wickedness. God, let not another build on their foundation of wickedness in the name of Jesus Christ according to Judges 7:20-22, Jer. 51:26.

God, send your all consuming fire to burn up and destroy everything that is in the atmosphere that has formed a snare, and barricade of wickedness of every level, rank, form, shape, time, and place that was released over our lives in the night season in the name of Jesus Christ according to Gen. 19:24,27, Acts 19:19, Amos 2:2-3.

But the LORD is with me as a mighty terrible one: therefore my persecutors shall stumble, and they shall not prevail: they shall be greatly ashamed; for they shall not prosper: their everlasting confusion shall never be forgotten.

But, O LORD of hosts that tryest the righteous, and seest the reins and the heart, let me see thy vengeance on them: for unto thee have I opened my cause. Sing unto the LORD, praise ye the LORD: for he hath delivered the soul of the poor from the hand of evildoers.

Whoso diggeth a pit, shall fall therein: and he that rolleth a stone, it will return upon him.

For the day of the LORD is near upon all the heathen: as thou hast done, it shall be done unto thee: thy reward shall return upon thine own head. For as ye have drunk upon my holy mountain, so shall all the heathen drink continually, yea, they shall drink, and they shall swallow down, and they shall be as though they had not been.

But upon mount Zion shall be deliverance, and there shall be holiness; and the house of Jacob shall possess their possessions. And the house of Jacob shall be a fire, and the house of Joseph a flame.

God we thank you and praise you for the speedy execution of this prayer in the name of Jesus Christ and we give you the praise, the glory, and the honor. Amen.

Warfare Prayer Against Backwardness

Father God in the name of Jesus Christ, we command fire to come down and destroy every spirit of backwardness programmed in our life, in the name of Jesus Christ according to Num 11:1.

God, release the wisdom to uncover and locate every door way that the enemy uses to infiltrate to form, and enforce these barriers of backwardness, causing stagnation, missed opportunities, procrastination, and poverty in our lives in the name of Jesus Christ. God, destroy with fire every barrier that has been planted with in our mind set, thought patterns, and belief system that is stopping and blocking us from getting an education, getting a degree, getting licensed, getting or setting appointments, and perusing opportunities in the name of Jesus Christ according to Duet 4:24. We release the judgment of God against every python spirit that has networked with fear, rejection, and arrested development to form a 3-fold cord of restraint on our lives in the name of Jesus Christ according to Psalm 6:10.

God, rip up and destroy every shackle caused by the sins of the Father in the name of Jesus Christ according to Lev 26:40-42, Job 24:19.

God, we repent for our sins and the sins of our fore fathers that have opened up the doors caused by the curse of illegitimacy in the name of Jesus Christ.

For if we confess our sins you are faithful and just to forgive us and the Blood of Jesus Christ will cleanse us from all unrighteousness. God, destroy every shackle and chain formed by curses, incantations, candle burning, ju ju's, hoodoo, voodoo, homemade witchcraft, grave yard curses, return all these works to the sender, oh God, destroy every barrier with fire in the name of Jesus Christ according to Act 19:19, Jer 51:58, Job 37:7.

Oh let the wickedness of the wicked come to an end; but establish the just: for the righteous God trieth the hearts and reins.

We bind up every strongman that enforces every type, level and form of barriers, collars, leashes, ropes, shackles, chains and yokes of backwardness, delay, and stagnation; we command your goods to be spoiled in the mighty name of Jesus Christ according to Mark 3:27.

We take the finger of Almighty God to locate and cast out every principality and power, and every demon that is assigned to enforce these satanic walls, shackles and yokes over our lives in the name of Jesus Christ according to Luke 11:20-22.

We command the hand of God to remove them out of their position of power according to 1Pet 3:22, Job 37:5-8.

God destroy with finger of God and the Blood of Jesus Christ every yoke and shackle caused by ancestral debt collectors in the name of Jesus Christ according to Luke 11:20-22, Mark 3:27.

God send the anointing to destroy every yoke of backwardness that has been formed by the enemy in the name of Jesus Christ according to Isaiah 10:27.

God we take the keys of the kingdom of God, that whatever we loose on earth shall be loosed in heaven, Jesus we loose ourselves from every shackle, fetter and chain in the name of Jesus Christ according to Matt 18:18 c.

God destroy with fire, every three fold cord of backwardness that has been programmed in my life in the name of Jesus Christ according to Judges 16:3.

God rip up every contract made by my ancestors that is planted in the heavenlies that acts as a barrier, yoke, and dog collar to hinder and stagnate every area of our lives in the name of Jesus Christ according to 2Cor 10:4.

God destroy every soul tie and blood line connection, with every person living or dead that has made a pact or contract through witchcraft over our lives and the lives of our descendents going back 70 generations, and going forward 3 to 4 generations in the name of Jesus Christ.

Destroy with fire and brimstone every family dedication made to satan in the name of Jesus Christ according to Gen 19:24, 27.
God rip up and erase every name on these contracts with the hand of God and the blood of Jesus Christ.

For the LORD shall fight for you, and ye shall hold your peace. And the LORD said unto Moses, Wherefore criest thou unto me? Speak unto the children of Israel, that they go forward. God, we ask that you speak to every situation that has been held up and stagnated by satanic forces we speak the word to go forward in the name of Jesus Christ.

We release Heavenly Judgment against every demonic activity assigned against my life in the name of Jesus Christ.

God we command the immediate destruction against every contract which has not been validated by the Lord Jesus Christ.

God put in our spirit, body and soul, mind, will and emotion the drive to go forward according to 2Kings 4:24; to break through in faith regardless of the situation and how things look.

For then shalt thou go on forward from thence, and thou shalt come to the plain of Tabor, and there shall you meet three men going up to God to Beth—el, one carrying three kids, and another carrying thee three loaves of bread, and another carrying a bottle of wine: And they will salute thee, and give thee two loaves of bread; which thou shalt receive of their hands.

God let us go forward and run into every person that is assigned to meet us along the way, to bless us, and to impart into us, and further us along the journey in the name of Jesus Christ according to 1Sam 10:3.

God let all the blessings and anointing that was held up to go forward with us, from this day forward according to 1Sam. 16:13.

God we ask that you reprogram us to go forward, to follow after and fulfill the will of God as you intended in the name of Jesus Christ according to Ezek 1:9.

God let us go forward as the spirit of God directs us, and to plow through the forces of the enemies according to Ezek 1:12.

God let us go forward into the place we need to be in the name of Jesus Christ according to 2Cor 8:10.

Lord Jesus, we thank you and praise you for being an adversary to every adversary of backwardness and delay in our lives according to Isaiah 49:24-26.

And God, we praise you for deliverance for you said upon Mount Zion there shall be deliverance.

We thank you Jesus, for chains being broken.

We thank you Jesus, for shackles being destroyed.

We thank you Jesus, for walls falling down flat.

We thank you Jesus, for contracts being ripped up and thrown in the fire by your mighty hands.

We thank you Jesus, for yokes being destroyed because of the anointing.

We thank you Jesus that every weapon that was formed against us will no longer prosper.

We bless your Holy name, we give you the glory, we praise you for our deliverance, we do give you the honor, for you have all power in heaven and in earth, we thank you for the turnaround in our lives, in the name of the Lord Jesus Christ.

O love the LORD, all ye his saints: *for* the LORD preserveth the faithful, and plentifully rewardeth the proud doer. Be of good courage, and he shall strengthen your heart, all ye that hope in the LORD. Amen.

Warfare Prayer to Release Fire

Father God in the name of Jesus Christ, destroy with fire any thing that was used to create any and every satanic barriers, shackles, and yokes over my life in the name of Jesus Christ according to Acts 19:19, Isaiah 10:27.

God, destroy with fire everything that was used to create satanic barriers around my finances in the name of Jesus Christ according to Jer 51:58.

God rip up and destroy with fire everything that the enemy has used to block the release of my blessings in the name of Jesus Christ.

God destroy with fire every pot and caldron that has initiated poverty over my life and blood line in the name of Jesus Christ according to Amos 2:2-3.

God take the key of David to close every door and destroy with fire everything that the enemy uses to gain access to enforce walls and barriers over my life in the name of Jesus Christ according to Rev 3:7.

God we ask that you locate and destroy with fire every curse, ritual, and enchantment that has been attached to my life by using any photograph with my likeness on it in the name of Jesus Christ according to Gen 19:24, 27.

God locate and destroy with fire every power of darkness used to sabotage my blessings in the name of Jesus Christ according to Duet 9:3.

I release the fire of God to destroy every barrier of limitations placed upon my life thru meditations, spoken word curses, spells, enchantments, (homemade) and Charismatic witchcraft in the name of Jesus Christ according to Acts 19:19, 1 Chron 4:10.

God destroy with fire every object planted in the heavens, and in the earth that was designed to stagnate and block the release of my prosperity in the name of Jesus Christ according to Jer 51:58.

God destroy with fire everything that has been designed to release sickness and poverty upon my life in the name of Jesus Christ according Duet. 7:5.

We curse the power, wisdom, and the success of every Baalam that has been hired to put curses on my life and my family, we call down fire from heaven to locate and destroy every known and unknown work of witchcraft released to oppress our lives, in the name of Jesus Christ according to Acts 19:19, Amos 2:2-3, Matt 13:41-42.

And Elijah answered and said to the captain of fifty, If I be a man of God, then let fire come down from heaven, and consume thee and thy fifty. And there came down fire from heaven, and consumed him and his fifty, according to 2Kings 1:10.

God locate and destroy with fire, every satanic and witchcraft contract, handwriting and ordinance of every type, level, order, rank, time, and place, that was taken out on my life in the name of Jesus Christ according to Acts 19:19, Joel 2:3.

God send fire 7 times hotter to destroy every type of bond that we are a prisoner to, in the name of Jesus Christ according to Dan 3:25-27.

God send fire to destroy every 3-fold cord in our life that is time released at the point of breakthrough in the name of Jesus Christ according to Judges 16:3.

God send fire to release your glory over our lives in the name of Jesus Christ according to Duet 5:24.

God open up the heavens by fire to fill us with your glory and your presence in the name of Jesus Christ of Nazareth.

God destroy by fire and brimstone every satanic canopy that is blocking the glory of God, from saturating my life in the name of the Lord Jesus Christ.

God we thank you and praise you for you said that you would baptize us with the Holy Ghost and with Fire in the name of Jesus Christ.

And God, we praise you for fire in our lives and over lives in Jesus Name. Amen.

Warfare Prayer to Be Loosed

Father God in the name of Jesus Christ, we repent for the kingdom of God has come nigh unto us. Shake thyself from the dust; arise, and sit down, O Jerusalem: loose thyself from the bands of thy neck, O captive daughter of Zion. For thus saith the LORD, Ye have sold yourselves for naught; and ye shall be redeemed without money.

God you said in Matt 18:18c, that what so ever we loose on earth shall be loosed in heaven.

Every person being hounded and monitored by witchcraft and demonic forces be loosed from every silver cord in the heavens and the earth in the name of Jesus Christ according to Ecc 12:6a.

For he hath looked down from the height of his sanctuary; from heaven did the LORD behold the earth; To hear the groaning of the prisoner; to loose those that are appointed to death.

We thank you for the King of kings loosening us from every demonic force in the heavens and in the earth in the name of Jesus Christ according to Psalm 105:20.

God let us be loosed from every type of sin, addiction, sickness and demonic powers that have us bound in the name of Jesus Christ according to Judges 15:14.

God loose us from all generational curses caused by idolatry in the name of Jesus Christ.

God loose us from generational curses caused by witchcraft, sorcery, and divination in the name of Jesus Christ according to Judges 15:14.

God we seek your hand to loose us from satanic oppression and captivity in the name of Jesus Christ according to Isaiah 51:14. Woman thou art loosed from thine infirmity in the name of Jesus Christ according to Luke 13:12.

God we ask for forgiveness of our sins and the sins of our fathers in the name of Jesus Christ according Lev 26:40-42.

God we repent for our parents and fore-parents and ask that you loose us from every curse of illegitimacy, of being born out of wedlock in the name of Jesus Christ.

God loose us from every spirit spouse, and marriage breaking spirit in the name of Jesus Christ according to Matt. 18:18c.

God loose us from every debt of every demonic and ancestral debt collector for oaths, pledges, and covenants made by our ancestors going back 70 generations on both sides of my family in the name of Jesus Christ according to Matt. 18:27.

God we ask that you loose us from all backwardness and stagnation in the name of Jesus Christ according to Matt. 18:18 c.

Father God in the name of Jesus Christ, we ask that you loose us from the spirit of excuses in the name of Jesus Christ.

God loose us from all mind control through witchcraft in the name of Jesus Christ according to Matt 18:18c.

God loose us from all MPD and arrested development in the name of Jesus Christ according to Matt 18:18c.

God loose us from all spoken word curses in the name of Jesus Christ according to Matt 18:18c.

God loose us from all Jezebelic prayers in the name of Jesus Christ according to Matt. 18:18c.

God loose us from every curse planted in the heavens in the name of Jesus Christ according to Matt 18:18c.

In the name of Jesus Christ, we loose every blessing that has been held up by satanic forces according to Matt 18:18c.

And at midnight Paul and Silas prayed, and sang praises unto God; and the prisoners heard them. And suddenly there was a great earthquake, so that the foundations of the prison were shaken; and immediately all the doors were opened, and every one's bands were loosed.

God we sing praises to you right now and we thank you for the earthquake that's going to loose everyone's bands in the name of Jesus Christ.

God we confess and repent for our sins and ask that you loose every blessing that was held up by our sins in the name of Jesus Christ according to 1John 1:7, 9.

God we repent for all unforgiveness that has tied up our blessings in the name of Jesus Christ.

God we ask that you loose healing and restoration in our lives in the name of Jesus Christ.

And God, we praise you loosening us from everything in earth and in the heavens that has not been sanction by the Lord Jesus Christ.

For thus saith the Lord, And now, behold, I loose thee this day from the chains which were upon thine hand according to Jer 40:4.

It is of the LORD'S mercies that we are not consumed, because his compassions fail not. *They are* new every morning: great *is* thy faithfulness. The LORD *is* my portion, saith my soul; therefore will I hope in him.

The LORD *is* good unto them that wait for him, to the soul *that* seeketh him. *It is* good that *a man* should both hope and quietly wait for the salvation of the LORD.

God as we wait, we anticipate the loosening of the bands of wickedness that has been placed on our lives in the name of Jesus Christ.

Thus sayeth the LORD to his anointed, to Cyrus, whose right hand I have holden, to subdue nations before him; and I will loose the loins of kings, to open before him the two leaved gates; and the gates shall not be shut.

I will go before thee, and make the crooked places straight: I will break in pieces the gates of brass, and cut in sunder the bars of iron. God, we bless you for the Cyrus anointing in the name of Yeshua Hamashiah.

Happy is he that hath the God of Jacob for his help, whose hope is in the LORD his God: which made heaven, and earth, the sea, and all that therein is: which keepeth truth forever. Which executeth judgment for the oppressed: which giveth food to the hungry. The LORD looseth the prisoners.

The LORD openeth the eyes of the blind: the LORD raiseth them that are bowed down: the LORD loveth the righteous.

The LORD preserveth the strangers; he relieveth the fatherless and widow: but the way of the wicked he turneth upside down.

The LORD shall reign forever, even thy God, O Zion, unto all generations. Praise ye the LORD.

The Warfare's Prayer

Father God in the name of Jesus Christ, I come against all wiccans, belials, new agers, hoodoos and voodoo doctors, witches, warlocks, satanist, Jezebel's that have released curses, spells, chants, hexes, and vexes against my health, ministry and finances in the night season in name of Jesus Christ according to Isaiah 44:25, Job 20:5-15.

For he hath swallowed down riches, and he shall vomit them up again: God shall cast them out of his belly. He shall suck the poison of asps: the viper's tongue shall slay him. He shall not see the rivers, the floods, the brooks of honey and butter.

That which he labored for shall he restore, and shall not swallow it down: according to his substance shall the restitution be, and he shall not rejoice therein.

God we curse their powers and their success, God strips them of their spirit guides, spirit helps, and personal attendants in the name of the Lord Jesus Christ according to Num 14:9.

God I curse their works and their success with the voice of the Lord Jesus Christ according to Mark 11:14, 20.

God I curse the power, wisdom, progress, and success of all the works of Charismatic Church witchcraft in the name of Jesus Christ, God with a blast from your nostrils I command the release of panic, havoc, confusion, backwardness, stagnation, destruction, torment, and paranoia to hunt down, locate, and manifest itself upon every person that has formed a group for secret attacks in the name of Jesus Christ according to Isaiah 19:14-16, Judges 7:20-22, Job 4:8-9.

For the wicked have drawn out the sword, and have bent their bow, to cast down the poor and needy, and to slay such as be of upright conversation. Their sword shall enter into their own heart, and their bows shall be broken.

God, I put all their works of witchcraft along with their attendants that have been released in the heavens in the hands of Alpha and Omega, God locate every one of them and snatch them out of the atmosphere and to be bond up and taken to tartartus in the name of Jesus Christ according 2Cor 10:4, Job 14:17, 2Pet. 2:4.

God wrap them up in the blood of Jesus Christ and move them out of their position of power in the name of Jesus Christ according to Exodus 33:2.

God lock them in Iron, fetters and everlasting chains according to Psalm 149:9-10, Jude 1:6.

God, we command these powers and works to loose their hold on what they have stolen in the name of Jesus Christ according Matt. 18:18c.

For the arms of the wicked shall be broken: but the LORD upholdeth the righteous.

I release the conquest of Canaan to gather up the spoils from the land of milk and honey; to rejoice and enjoy houses we have not build and vineyards we have not planted in the name of Jesus Christ.

Oh let the wickedness of the wicked come to an end; but establish the just: for the righteous God trieth the hearts and reins.

The heavens shall reveal his iniquity; and the earth shall rise up against him. The increase of his house shall depart, and his goods shall flow away in the day of his wrath.

This is the portion of a wicked man and (woman) from God, and the heritage appointed unto him by God.

God we thank you for you are God and God alone, and your name is Great and you are greatly to be praised, and your name is holy, and we give you the glory and honor in the name of Yeshua Hamashiah. Amen.

Releasing the Power of the Destroyer

Father God in the name of Jesus Christ, we repent for the kingdom of God has come nigh unto us; God, if the reader of this prayer is not right in their heart then let this be counted as a sin against them in the name of Jesus Christ.

God we ask that you cover us, our family, church, ministry, business, and job in the Blood of the lamb according to Exodus 12:23.

We release the Destroyer (the Shachath) against every spirit of sickness, poverty, and disease that is caused by generational curses in the name of Jesus Christ.

The wicked man travaileth with pain all his days, and the number of years is hidden to the oppressor. A dreadful sound is in his ears: in prosperity the destroyer shall come upon him.

God let this be the portion of every witch, warlock, balaam, belial, jezebel, Satanist, sorcerer, hoodoo, voodoo practitioner, their spirit guides and spirit helps, attendants and cohorts in the natural and in the spirit in the name of Jesus Christ according to Job 15:20-21.

God we release the Destroyer (the Shachath) to hunt down and locate with relentless pursuit every person that has put curses and released bounty's on every facet of our lives in the name of Jesus Christ.

For thus saith the LORD to the men of Judah and Jerusalem: Break up your fallow ground, and sow not among thorns. Circumcise yourselves to the LORD, and take away the foreskins of your heart, ye men of Judah and inhabitants of Jerusalem: lest my fury come forth like fire, and burn that none can quench it, because of the evil of your doings.

Declare ye in Judah, and publish in Jerusalem; and say, Blow ye the trumpet in the land; cry, gather together, and say, Assemble yourselves, and let us go into the defenced cities. Set up the standard toward Zion; retire, stay not: for I will bring evil from the north, and a great destruction.

The lion is come up from his thicket, and the destroyer of the Gentiles is on his way; he is gone forth from his place to make thy land desolate; and thy cities shall be laid waste, without an inhabitant.

God let this be the portion against every antichrist that is coming against the church and the furthering of the Gospel in the name of Jesus Christ.

And God, we ask that you anoint us as you did Samson to be a Destroyer to every philistine in our lives in the natural and in the spirit in the name of Jesus Christ according to Judges 16:24.

God anoint our prayers, our praise, and our worship to be a Destroyer against everything that has not been sanctioned by the Lord Jesus Christ; and God, we praise you and we magnify you in the name of Jesus Christ.

God, we release the Destroyer (the Shachath) against every spirit of Backwardness, stagnation, sabotage, delay, trickery and deception that has been assigned to our lives through (Charismatic) witchcraft in the name of Jesus Christ.

God, we release the Destroyer against every prophetic satanic utterance and meditation released from Jezebel and the children of Belial in the name of Jesus Christ.

The LORD is known by the judgment which he executeth: the wicked is snared in the work of his own hands. Higgaion. Selah. The wicked shall be turned into hell, and all the nations that forget God.

For the needy shall not always be forgotten: the expectation of the poor shall not perish forever.

Arise, O LORD; let not man prevail: let the heathen be judged in thy sight. Put them in fear, O LORD: that the nations may know themselves to be but men. Selah; and God we give you the praise in the name of Jesus Christ. Amen.

Prayer to Release the Spirit of Judgment and Burning

Father God in the name of Jesus Christ, we release the spirit of Judgment and burning in the name of Jesus Christ. And it shall come to pass, that he that is left in Zion, and he that remaineth in Jerusalem, shall be called holy, even every one that is written among the living in Jerusalem.

When the Lord shall have washed away the filth of the daughters of Zion, and shall have purged the blood of Jerusalem from the midst thereof by the spirit of judgment, and by the spirit of burning.

God, we confess and ask that you wash away the filth of our sins and iniquities, and throw them as far as the east is from the west in the name of Jesus Christ.

God as you judge us first, we ask you for mercy so that you would also judge our enemies according to your righteousness in the name of Jesus Christ.

Thou hast a mighty arm: strong is thy hand, and high is thy right hand. Justice and judgment are the habitation of thy throne: mercy and truth shall go before thy face.

The LORD shall judge the people: judge me, O LORD, according to my righteousness, and according to mine integrity that is in me. Oh let the wickedness of the wicked come to an end; but establish the just: for the righteous God trieth the hearts and reins.

But I will send a fire upon Moab, and it shall devour the palaces of Kerioth: and Moab shall die with tumult, with shouting, and with the sound of the trumpet: And I will cut off the judge from the midst thereof, and will slay all the princes thereof with him, sayeth the LORD.

Let the saints be joyful in glory: let them sing aloud upon their beds.

Let the high praises of God be in their mouth, and a two-edged sword in their hand; To execute vengeance upon the heathen, and punishments upon the people; To bind their kings with chains, and their nobles with fetters of iron; To execute upon them the judgment written: this honor have all his saints.

The name of the LORD is a strong tower: the righteous runneth into it, and is safe. I have done judgment and justice: leave me not to mine oppressors. Be surety for thy servant for good: let not the proud oppress me.

The heathen are sunk down in the pit that they made: in the net which they hid is their own foot taken. The LORD is known by the judgment which he executeth: the wicked is snared in the work of his own hands in the name of Jesus Christ.

O LORD: keep not silence: O Lord, be not far from me. Stir up thyself, and awake to my judgment, even unto my cause, my God and my Lord. Judge me, O LORD my God, according to thy righteousness; and let them not rejoice over me.

Let them not say in their hearts, Ah, so would we have it: let them not say, We have swallowed him up. Let them be ashamed and brought to confusion together that rejoice at mine hurt; let them be clothed with shame and dishonor that magnify themselves against me.

Commit thy way unto the LORD; trust also in him; and he shall bring it to pass. And he shall bring forth thy righteousness as the light, and thy judgment as the noonday. Rest in the LORD, and wait patiently for him: fret not thyself because of him who prospereth in his way, because of the man who bringeth wicked devices to pass.

Cease from anger, and forsake wrath: fret not thyself in any wise to do evil. For evildoers shall be cut off: but those that wait upon the LORD, they shall inherit the earth. For yet a little while, and the wicked shall not be: yea, thou shalt diligently consider his place, and it shall not be.

For the LORD loveth judgment, and forsaketh not his saints; they are preserved for ever: but the seed of the wicked shall be cut off.

O LORD God of our fathers, art not thou God in heaven? And rulest not thou over all the kingdoms of the heathen? And in thine hand is there not power and might, so that none is able to withstand thee?

Art not thou our God, who didst drive out the inhabitants of this land before thy people Israel, and gavest it to the seed of Abraham thy friend forever? And they dwelt therein, and have built thee a sanctuary therein for thy name, saying, If, when evil cometh upon us, as the sword, judgment, or pestilence, or famine, we stand before this house, and in thy presence, (for thy name is in this house,) and cry unto thee in our affliction, then thou wilt hear and help.

And now, behold, the children of Ammon and Moab and mount Seir, whom thou wouldest not let Israel invade, when they came out of the land of Egypt, but they turned from them, and destroyed them not; Behold, I say, how they reward us, to come to cast us out of thy possession, which thou hast given us to inherit. Oh God, wilt thou not judge them? For we have no might against this great company that cometh against us; neither know we what to do: but our eyes are upon thee.

God, our eyes are upon thee for you are great, and you ruleth over our enemies. God, execute your righteous judgment against every type of witchcraft, spoken word curses, Jezebelic prayers, hoodoo, voodoo, charismatic witchcraft, homemade witchcraft, wiccan magic, astral altars, Satanism, ancestral debt collectors, necromancy, and satanic oaths, pledges and family dedications of every sort, level, order, rank, time and, place in the name of Jesus Christ.

The stouthearted are spoiled, they have slept their sleep: and none of the men of might have found their hands. At thy rebuke, O God of Jacob, both the chariot and horse are cast into a dead sleep. Vow, and pay unto the LORD your God: let all that be round about him bring presents unto him that ought to be feared. He shall cut off the spirit of princes; he is terrible to the kings of the soil.

The LORD executeth righteousness and judgments for all that are oppressed. He made known his ways unto Moses, his acts unto the children of Israel. How many are the days of thy servant? When wilt thou execute judgment on them that persecute me? For God shall bring every work into judgment, with every secret thing, whether it be good, or whether it be evil.

God, we praise and we bless your Holy name, for mercy and judgment are you habitation, we glorify you for your majesty oh King of Kings, and we praise you in the name of Yeshua Hamashiah Amen!!!!!

Destroying Curses That Transfer
Our Blessings and Inheritance

Father God in the name of Jesus Christ, we destroy with fire every power that has transferred and hijacked my blessings to another person in the name of Jesus Christ according to Job 37:7-8, Acts 19:19, and Duet. 7:5.

Ask of me, and I shall give *thee* the heathen *for* thine inheritance, and the uttermost parts of the earth *for* thy possession. Thou shalt break them with a rod of iron; thou shalt dash them in pieces like a potter's vessel, in the name of Jesus Christ.

God, destroy with fire every work of witchcraft that has been programmed to hijack my blessings to another person in the name of Jesus Christ according to Joel 2:3, Amos 2:2-3, Acts 19:19, and Duet. 12:3.

Thus saith the LORD, thy redeemer, and he that formed thee from the womb, I am the LORD that maketh all things; that stretcheth forth the heavens alone; that spreadeth abroad the earth by myself; that frustrateth the tokens of the liars, and maketh diviners mad; that turneth wise men backward, and maketh their knowledge foolish.

God, send your warrior angels to locate, rip up, reverse, make null and void and destroy every contract, hand writing and ordinance made that has been planted and specially designed in the heavens to transfer my blessings to another person in the name of Jesus Christ according to 2 Cor. 10:4, Matt. 13:41-42.

God, thundereth marvelously with his voice; great things doeth he, which we cannot comprehend. For he saith to the snow, Be thou *on* the earth; likewise to the small rain, and to the great rain of his strength. He sealeth up the hand of every man; that all men may know his work. Then the beasts go into dens, and remain in their places.

God, seal up the works of every hand of the enemy that has released orders, and curses to transfer my blessings, and every beast that has patrolled and enforced this in the spirit in the name of Jesus Christ according to Job 37:6-8.

For the wicked in his pride doth persecute the poor: let them be taken in the devices that they have imagined.

God, send your angels to locate and bind in everlasting chains, every python, every spiritual thief, and every ancestral debt collector that has robbed me of my blessings, we command the judgment of tartartus to locate and bind every one of them in everlasting chains, to overtake them and make every demon reaper and evil spirit to cough up, release, and return my blessings to its proper time and place in the name of Jesus Christ according to 2Pet. 2:4, Job 20:15.

God, destroy with fire and remove with the blood of Jesus Christ the mark of every imposter that the enemy has set up to receive my blessings in the name of Jesus Christ according to Lev. 9:24.

God, demote every person and power assigned to hijack and transfer my blessings in the name of Jesus Christ according to Isaiah 14:10, Oba. 4, Num. 14:9, Num. 24:11.

Oh let the wickedness of the wicked come to an end; but establish the just: for the righteous God trieth the hearts and reins.

God, let ever blessing that was stolen be returned to me with God speed; for God you said, And I will restore to you the years that the locust hath eaten, the cankerworm, and the caterpillar, and the palmerworm, my great army which I sent among you. And ye shall eat in plenty, and be satisfied, and praise the name of the LORD your God that hath dealt wondrously with you: and my people shall never be ashamed.

God, as David encouraged himself, we do also and rest in the fact of your word that you said Pursue: for thou shalt surely overtake *them*, and without fail recover *all,* God we send up violent prayers and praises to pursue after every stolen blessing; God we recover all without fail everything that every spiritual amalekite has taken and we decree and declare nothing was missing small or great according to 1Sam. 30:18-19.

God, we release these petitions in your heavenly court room for you are THE RIGHTOEUS JUDGE and we thank you for the reversal and cancelation of every executed order that has not been given approval by the Lord Jesus Christ, in the name of the Jesus Christ. That thou mayest give him rest from the days of adversity, until the pit be digged for the wicked. For the LORD will not cast off his people, neither will he forsake his inheritance.

God, we praise you for the Shock and Awe and the immediate destruction of the enemies forces according to Jer. 51:58, Num. 14:9, Psalm 68:17, Matt. 13:41-42.

He hath swallowed down riches, and he shall vomit them up again: God shall cast them out of his belly. He shall suck the poison of asps: the viper's tongue shall slay him. He shall not see the rivers, the floods, the brooks of honey and butter.

That which he labored for shall he restore, and shall not swallow *it* down: according to *his* substance *shall* the restitution *be,* and he shall not rejoice *therein.*

Because he hath oppressed *and* hath forsaken the poor; *because* he hath violently taken away an house which he buildeth not; Surely he shall not feel quietness in his belly, he shall not save of that which he desired. There shall none of his meat be left; therefore shall no man look for his goods.

In the fullness of his sufficiency he shall be in straits: every hand of the wicked shall come upon him. *When* he is about to fill his belly, *God* shall cast the fury of his wrath upon him, and shall rain *it* upon him while he is eating.

In the year of the jubilee the field shall return unto him of whom it was bought, *even* to him to whom the possession of the land *did belong*.

God, we thank you for the restoration of blessings; for blessed *be* the God and Father of our Lord Jesus Christ, who hath blessed us with all spiritual blessings in heavenly *places* in Christ.

Lord God, we thank you for this special Jubilee for the return of our possessions, and we give you the praise for the restoration of both spiritual and natural blessings in the name of Jesus Christ for you said, "I will return unto thee according to the time of life."
And God we thank you for the promise that is in your word; we send up praises, we bless your holy name for you are God and God alone.

We thank you Lord God, for you are not a man you should lie, nor the son of man you should repent, and we praise the Lord for his mercy endureth forever.

And God, we give you thanks in the name of Yeshua Hamashiah. Amen.

Warfare Prayer to Release Spoilers

Father God in the name of Jesus Christ, we repent for the kingdom of God has come nigh unto us. God, you said if we confess our sins you are faithful and just to forgive us and the blood of Jesus Christ shall cleanse us from all unrighteousness.

Shall the prey be taken from the mighty, or the lawful captive delivered? But thus saith the LORD, Even the captives of the mighty shall be taken away, and the prey of the terrible shall be delivered: for I will contend with him that contendeth with thee, and I will save thy children. And I will feed them that oppress thee with their own flesh; and they shall be drunken with their own blood, as with sweet wine: and all flesh shall know that I the LORD am thy Savior and thy Redeemer, the mighty One of Jacob.

Father God in the name of Jesus Christ, we thank you for spoiling and plundering the goods of every strong man that is assigned to our family and our entire bloodline in the name of Jesus Christ according to Mark 3:27.

We release the finger of God to hunt down, locate, over power, and overthrow every strong man and the devises that have been devised against our lives, family, business, and ministry in the name of Jesus Christ according to Exodus 8:19, Luke 11:20-22.

Behold, therefore I will stretch out mine hand upon thee, and will deliver thee for a spoil to the heathen; and I will cut thee off from the people, and I will cause thee to perish out of the countries: I will destroy thee; and thou shalt know that I *am* the LORD. God, let this be the portion of every person that has targeted our lives, family, business, ministry, health and church through witchcrafts and whoredoms in the name of Jesus Christ.

Arise, get you up unto the wealthy nation, that dwelleth without care, saith the LORD, which have neither gates nor bars, which dwell alone. And their camels shall be a booty , and the multitude of their cattle a spoil: and I will scatter into all winds them that are in the utmost corners; and I will bring their calamity from all sides thereof, saith the LORD according to Jer 49:31-32.

God we release our prayers, praise and worship to go forward and spoil those who have spoiled us, and to rob those who have robed us in the name of Jesus Christ according to Ezek 39:10.

Wherefore, behold, the days come, saith the LORD, that I will do judgment upon her graven images: and through all her land the wounded shall groan. Though Babylon should mount up to heaven, and though she should fortify the height of her strength.

Yet from me shall spoilers come unto her, saith the LORD. A sound of a cry cometh from Babylon, and great destruction from the land of the Chaldeans: Because the LORD hath spoiled Babylon, and destroyed out of her the great voice; when her waves do roar like great waters, a noise of their voice is uttered.

Because the spoiler is come upon her, even upon Babylon, and her mighty men are taken, every one of their bows is broken: for the LORD God of recompenses shall surely requite. And I will make drunk her princes, and her wise men, her captains, and her rulers, and her mighty men: and they shall sleep a perpetual sleep, and not wake, saith the King, whose name is the LORD of hosts.

Lord Jesus, we praise you for thy Kingdom come and thy will be done on earth as it is in heaven!!!

God, send your sword and your spoilers to hunt down, locate, and devour from within the second heavens and the earth's realm all those that have spoiled us in the name of Jesus Christ according to Jer. 12:12.

When (the wicked) shall be judged, let him be condemned: and let his prayer become sin. Let his days be few.

Let there be none to extend mercy unto him. Let them be before the LORD continually that he may cut off the memory of them from the earth.

God let this be the breakfast, lunch, dinner, and midnight snack to all those that have sought us, and that will seek us and our family members as a spoil; and to those who take up the office of their predecessors in the name of Jesus Christ.

But the LORD is with me as a mighty terrible one: therefore my persecutors shall stumble, and they shall not prevail: they shall be greatly ashamed; for they shall not prosper: their everlasting confusion shall never be forgotten.

But, O LORD of hosts, that tryest the righteous, and seest the reins and the heart, let me see thy vengeance on them: for unto thee have I opened my cause. Sing unto the LORD, praise ye the LORD: for he hath delivered the soul of the poor from the hand of evildoers.

Let this entire prayer hunt down, locate and seal itself around every person, group and confederacy, let it be magnified 7 times 7 against all who have, and will sanction a bounty against us, and upon all who will take up a mantle to spoil us, and to conspire against us in the name of the Lord Jesus Christ, Amen.

Warfare Prayer Against Blood Line Curses

Father God in the name of Jesus Christ of Nazareth, God deliver me from all my transgressions according to Psalm 39:8. God send fire 7 times hotter as in Dan. 3:19; as the fire burned the bonds off Shadrach, Meshach, Abednego, Lord we repent for the Kingdom of God has come nigh unto us. God, we confess the sins, trespasses, iniquities, rebellion, idolatry, passivity, unbelief, unforgiveness, gossip, loshon, hora, sexual immorality, slander, false witness, lying tongue, wicked imagination, sowing discord, not tithing consistently.

Now God, go through our blood line from cavalry to this very moment. Lord, we confess the sins, the iniquities, the trespasses, and the ignorance and disobedience of our selves our foremothers and forefathers going back 42 generations according to Lev. 26:40-42; for you said if we shall confess our iniquity, and the iniquity of our fathers, with their trespass that they have trespassed against you, and that also they have walked contrary unto you, and that you have also walked contrary unto them, and have brought them (us) into the land of their enemies; if then their uncircumcised heart be humbled, and then they accept the punishment of their iniquity: then will I remember my covenant with Jacob and also my covenant with Isaac, and also my covenant with Abraham will I remember; and I will remember the land.

God, even though this is a general confession, honor our faith according to your word. God, purge our blood line with the blood of Jesus Christ. We release confusion, chaos, destruction, panic, havoc, disasters upon every confederacy policing our blood line, in the name of Jesus Christ.

God, send your angels with everlasting chains according Psalm 103:20; to bind up every strongman, every policing demon, every demonic enforcer, all demon drones, all imps that bring in military enforcement, demon reapers that down load information in the spirit realm, winged shadow demons that are responsible for network communication, attacks, backlash, retaliation, sabotage and booby traps and all demonic door and gate keepers and we spoil their goods, according to Matt. 18:18, Mark 3:27.

We bind up every spirit of generational poverty and failure in the name of Jesus Christ.

We bind in everlasting chains Olet the spirit of fear and poverty, Carnivorous the demon of mishandling money, and every demon that would cut holes in our pockets, wallets, purse, bank accounts, debit and credit cards. We bind these spirits in everlasting chains and drown them in the blood of Jesus Christ.

We release the blood of Jesus Christ and the fire of the Holy Ghost to fill up every hole that the devil has designed for our money to fall through in the name of Jesus Christ.

We release the judgment of God against every spirit that would illegally reinstate curses to open and keep open door ways for attacks of financial affliction and oppression on our family, destiny, ministry, finances, property and possessions, seeing it is a righteous thing for God to recompense tribulation to them that trouble you according to 2Thes. 1:6. We repent and take the key of David and close every door at the point of entry in the name of Jesus Christ according to Rev. 3:7.

God, we repent and ask that you break every curse including the curse of the Bastard in the name of Jesus Christ. For Gal. 3:13 says, Christ have redeemed us from the curse of the law, being made a curse for us. For it is written, cursed is everyone that hangeth from a tree.

God, according to 1John 1:7, 9; If we confess our sins you are faithful and just to forgive us and the Blood of Jesus Christ will cleanse us. Jesus, send your blood, the same Blood that spilled on Calvary, through our bloodline like a tsunami tidal wave in the name of Jesus Christ.

Now God send fire 7 times hotter and even as fire and brimstone destroyed Sodom and Gomorrah according to Gen. 19:24. Let fire and brimstone rain and destroy every family curse and works of witchcraft, and divination going through our Blood line.

God, send Angels with everlasting chains to bind up every demon of legalism operating, according to 2Pet. 2:4.

Jesus, hear my prayer oh Lord and give ear to this request, and God we thank you for the change for destroying all hereditary sicknesses, diseases and conditions.

Lord God we bless you and give you the praise in the name of Jesus Christ. Amen.

Releasing the Power of
The Blood of Jesus Christ

Father God in the name of Jesus Christ, God, we first thank you and praise you for the salvation, grace and power of the finished works of the cross, God, we thank you for Calvary and we bless you for your Blood that was shed in the name of Jesus Christ.

If they shall confess their iniquity, and the iniquity of their fathers, with their trespass which they trespassed against me, and that also they have walked contrary unto me. And that I also have walked contrary unto them, and have brought them into the land of their enemies; if then their uncircumcised hearts be humbled, and they then accept of the punishment of their iniquity: Then will I remember my covenant with Jacob, and also my covenant with Isaac, and also my covenant with Abraham will I remember; and I will remember the land.

God, we bless you for the atonement power that is in the Blood of the Lamb for God you became a curse for us for it is written cursed is he that hangeth from a tree.

God ,we take the Blood of Jesus Christ and release it like a tsunami tidal wave going through our blood line from now all the way back to Adam and Eve to close every door way at the point of entry and the point of exit in the name of Jesus Christ.

Jesus, we take your precious blood and apply it over the lintel and the door posts of our home, business, ministry, family, health and finances in the name of Jesus Christ according to Exodus 12:7.

And the blood shall be to you for a token upon the houses where ye are: and when I see the blood, I will pass over you, and the plague shall not be upon you to destroy you, when I smite the land of Egypt according to Exodus 12:13.

God, we thank you for the Blood over our lives as the destroyer is released to slay every Pharaoh and his Egyptian cohorts that is over our lives that has made an alliance with our ancestral spirits to keep us in physical, spiritual, mental and financial bondage in the name of Jesus Christ according to Exodus 12:23.

God, send the destroyer to hunt down, capture and bind in everlasting chains made out of the blood of Jesus Christ ever evil spirit, python spirit, dark angel, and ancestral spirit that is operating physical, spiritual, mental and financial oppression against us from the second heavens in the name of Jesus Christ according to 2Pet. 2:4.

God, we release your warrior angels with swords, chains, battle axes, and battering rams formed and fashioned out of the Blood of Jesus Christ to demolish and destroy every barrier, snare and barricade that has been has been constructed in the second heavens to stop, block, hinder and delay every blessing, and promise that God has ordained for our lives in the name of Jesus Christ according 2Cor. 10:4.

God, have your angels to mount up with weapons of war fashioned out of the blood of Jesus Christ to fight against every works of witchcraft, hoodoo, voodoo, chants, spells, hexes, vexes, astral projections, Jezebelic prayers and psychic meditations that were sent in the night season. God, send your angels after the order of Sisera in the name of Jesus Christ according to Judges 5:20.

We release angels that are bounty hunters to hunt down and bind in everlasting chains made out of the blood of Jesus Christ every spirit spouse, marriage breaking spirit, spirit of infirmities, spirits of premature death, spirits of poverty, spirits of misfortune caused by curses, hexes, vexes, and the sins of our fathers in the name of Jesus Christ.

God let our oppressors that have taken up arms against us be drowned in the red sea as the Egyptians in the name of Jesus Christ.

God let the Blood of Jesus Christ flow like a tidal wave in the second heavens to destroy ever astral altar, pot, and caldron, and all curses, hexes, contracts and spells that have been planted in the heavens around my star in the name of Jesus Christ.

God we bind in everlasting chains all of their spiritual attendants, guides and spies in the blood of Jesus Christ.

God we release the fear of The Lord and the Blood of Jesus Christ against all of our enemies in the name of Jesus Christ.

God we Command your archers to send arrows made out of the blood of Jesus Christ into the hearts of our enemies and into the souls of the spirits they have summoned to bring oppression upon our health, finances and family in the name of Jesus Christ.

God we ask that the blood of Jesus Christ rain down on everything that is connected to wickedness that has connected to our lives. God, rain down the blood of the lamb on every work of spiritual oppression that the enemy has planted in the heavens and the earth against our blood line in the name of Jesus Christ according to Gen. 7:12.

God let the blood of the lamb rain down like in the days of Noah upon every stronghold and snare that the enemy has hidden. God, let the blood of Jesus Christ rain down and drown every secret council of the wicked in the heavens and the earth, and in the high places and in the realm of astral projection that is seeking after my soul in the name of Jesus Christ according to Gen. 7:12.

God we release the blood of Jesus Christ to bind up and choke every python, and strong man, Holy Ghost choke him until he coughs up what he has stolen in the name of Jesus Christ according to Mark 3:27.

God we ask that you inject the blood of Jesus Christ into our blood line to close up every open door caused by the curse of illegitimacy in the name of Jesus Christ.

God we ask that you inject the blood of Jesus Christ into our veins to destroy every blood line curse, sickness and disease that is hereditary or planted through witchcraft in the name of Jesus Christ.

God let the blood of the Lord Jesus Christ be injected in our blood line and veins to restore us to divine health in the name of Jesus Christ.

Purge us with hyssop so we can be clean wash us so we can be whiter than snow, God wash us and cleanse us oh God from all filthiness and Lord God we give you the praise in the name of Jesus Christ. Amen.

Releasing the Power of the Kingdom

Father God in the name of Jesus Christ we repent for the kingdom of God has come nigh unto us; for our Father who art in Heaven hallowed be thy name thy kingdom come thy will be done on earth as it is in heaven.

God, we ask that your kingdom would come in full power and might in the name of Yeshua Hamashiah, for it is the Father's good pleasure to give us the kingdom.

Now therefore, if ye will obey my voice indeed, and keep my covenant, then ye shall be a peculiar treasure unto me above all people; for all the earth is mine. And ye shall be unto me a kingdom of priests, and a holy nation. God, we repent and confess all sin so that we can be your peculiar treasure in the name of Jesus Christ according Exodus 19:5-6.

God we rejoice for the renewing of Kingdom in our lives in the name of Jesus Christ according to 1Sam 11:14-15.

God we ask that you establish the Kingdom of God in our hand in the name of Jesus Christ according to 2Chron. 17:5.

We release the power of the Kingdom to hunt down, locate, and vex all of our enemies in the name of Jesus Christ according to 1Sam. 14:47-48.

God we release the power of the kingdom against all of our sworn enemies and the enemies of God in the name of Jesus Christ. Thine arrows are sharp in the heart of the king's enemies; whereby the people fall under thee in the name of Jesus Christ according to Psalm 45:5.

For God you said, I will shake the heavens and the earth; and I will overthrow the throne of kingdoms; and I will destroy the strength of the kingdoms of the heathen; and I will overthrow the chariots, and those that ride in them; and the horses and their riders shall come down, everyone by the sword of his brother.

God, we seal this in the bowels of every witch, warlock, belial, and Anti-Christ, those that have set up a kingdom, that would oppose the kingdom of God, HIS Anointed, the church, and the Gospel of the Lord Jesus Christ according to Hag. 2:22, Num. 32:33.

For it is written at the name of Jesus Christ, every knee shall bow and every tongue shall confess that Jesus Christ is Lord.

God, give us as an inheritance the Kingdoms that you have over thrown in the name of Jesus Christ according to Josh. 12-14.

Of the increase of his government and peace there shall be no end, upon the throne of David, and upon his kingdom, to order it, and to establish it with judgment and with justice from henceforth even forever. The zeal of the LORD of hosts will perform this in the name of Yeshua Hamashiah.

And the seventh angel sounded and there were great voices in heaven. Saying, The kingdoms of this world are become the kingdoms of our Lord, and of his Christ; and he shall reign forever and ever.

And the four and twenty elders, which sat before God on their seats, fell upon their faces, and worshipped God, Saying, We give thee thanks, O Lord God Almighty, which art, and wast, and art to come; because thou hast taken to thee thy great power, and hast reigned.

The meek shall eat and be satisfied; they shall praise the LORD that seek him; your heart shall live forever. All the ends of the world shall remember and turn unto the LORD: and all the kindreds of the nations shall worship before thee. For the kingdom *is* the LORD'S: and he *is* the governor among the nations.

The LORD is good to all: and his tender mercies are over all his works. All thy works shall praise thee, O LORD; and thy saints shall bless thee. They shall speak of the glory of thy kingdom, and talk of thy power; to make known to the sons of men his mighty acts, and the glorious majesty of his kingdom.

Thy kingdom is an everlasting kingdom, and thy dominion endureth throughout all generations. The LORD upholdeth all that fall, and raiseth up all those that be bowed down. The eyes of all wait upon thee; and thou givest them their meat in due season. Thou openest thine hand, and satisfiest the desire of every living thing.

The LORD is righteous in all his ways and holy in all his works. The LORD is nigh unto all them that call upon him, to all that call upon him in truth. He will fulfill the desire of them that fear him: he also will hear their cry, and will save them. The LORD preserveth all them that love him: but all the wicked will he destroy. My mouth shall speak the praise of the LORD: and let all flesh bless his holy name forever and ever according to Psalm 145:9-21.

For he must reign, till he hath put all enemies under his feet. The last enemy *that* shall be destroyed *is* death. For he hath put all things under his feet. But when he saith all things are put under *him, it is* manifest that he is accepted, which did put all things under him.

And when all things shall be subdued unto him, then shall the Son also himself be subject unto him that put all things under him that God may be all in all according to 1Cor. 15:25-28.

And after these things I heard a great voice of much people in heaven, saying, Hallelujah; Salvation, and glory, and honor, and power, unto the Lord our God.

For true and righteous are his judgments: for he hath judged the great whore, which did corrupt the earth with her fornication, and hath avenged the blood of his servants at her hand. And again they said, Hallelujah. And her smoke rose up forever and ever.

And the four and twenty elders and the four beasts fell down and worshipped God that sat on the throne, saying, Amen. Hallelujah.

Wherefore we receiving a kingdom which cannot be moved, let us have grace, whereby we may serve God acceptably with reverence and godly fear: For our God is a consuming fire.

Now God, we thank you for the continual and eternal manifestation of the power and glory of your Kingdom in the earth realm and, God, we give you the praise in the name of Yeshua Hamashiah. Amen.

Warfare Prayer Releasing the Sword of the Lord

Father God in the name of Jesus Christ, before we wage war and go into battle we repent for the kingdom of God has come nigh unto us. God, we forgive those that need to be forgiven in the name of Jesus Christ. God, we renounce, repent and forsake our sins in the name of Jesus Christ.

Righteous art thou, O LORD, when I plead with thee: yet let me talk with thee of thy judgments: Wherefore doth the way of the wicked prosper? Wherefore are all they happy that deal very treacherously? Thou hast planted them, yea, they have taken root: they grow, yea, they bring forth fruit.

Thou are not near in their mouth, and far from their reins. But thou, O LORD, knowest me: thou hast seen me, and tried mine heart toward thee: pull them out like sheep for the slaughter, and prepare them for the day of slaughter in the name of Jesus Christ.

God, as we put on the whole armor of God, we call on the sword of the spirit which is the word of God in the name of Yeshua Hamashiah.

We shout the sword of the Lord and of Gideon in the name of Jesus Christ.

And all the host of heaven shall be dissolved, and the heavens shall be rolled together as a scroll: and all their hosts shall fall down, as the leaf falleth off from the vine and as a falling fig from the fig tree. For my sword shall be bathed in heaven: behold, it shall come down upon Idumea, and upon the people of my curse, to judgment.

God, we release the sword of the Lord on all workers of iniquity and spiritual wickedness in high places that have targeted us, we release your indignation to hunt down and to locate all works of witchcraft, their spirit guides, spirit helps, informants, attendants, their power, their knowledge, their discernment that they use to target our lives, family, business, ministry, anointing, and the purpose and the plan that God has for our lives in the name of Jesus Christ according to Isaiah 34:2-6.

In the name of Jesus Christ we take the Sword of the Lord to pursue and hunt down and slay the works, spirit guides, helps, wisdom and anointing of every Balaam and Jezebel that is sitting in the high places that is plotting, planning and assigning attacks against every facet of every purpose and plan that is the will of God for our lives in the name of Jesus Christ according to Num. 22:31, Josh. 13:22.

God, we take the Sword of the Lord, the anointing of Jehu and the zeal of Jehoiada to hunt down and slay every descendant of Ahab and Jezebel in the name of Jesus Christ according to 2Kings 11:20.

We take the sword of the Lord and slay the voice, command, and authority of every Rabshakeh that is releasing curses against your anointed in the earth realm for Thus saith the LORD, Be not afraid of the words that thou hast heard, wherewith the servants of the king of Assyria have blasphemed me.

Behold, I will send a blast upon him, and he shall hear a rumor, and return to his own land; and I will cause him to fall by the sword in his own land. God, let them fall by the sword now in the name of Jesus Christ according to Isaiah 37:6-7.

Now we thank you for the power and the anointing that is in your Sword; for in that day the LORD with his sore and great and strong sword shall punish leviathan the piercing serpent, even leviathan that crooked serpent; and he shall slay the dragon that is in the sea. God, we thank you for slaying spiritual oppositions that are greater than us in the name of Jesus Christ.

God, let the very letter of your word perform that which is written within this prayer in the name of Jesus Christ

There is none like unto the God of Jeshurun, who rideth upon the heaven in thy help, and in his Excellency on the sky. The eternal God is thy refuge, and underneath are the everlasting arms: and he shall thrust out the enemy from before thee; and shall say, Destroy them. Israel then shall dwell in safety alone: the fountain of Jacob shall be upon a land of corn and wine; also his heavens shall drop down dew.

Happy art thou, O Israel: who is like unto thee, O people saved by the LORD, the shield of thy help, and who is the sword of thy Excellency! And thine enemies shall be found liars unto thee; and thou shalt tread upon their high places.

God, we thank you. For you said; If ye walk in my statutes, and keep my commandments, and do them; then I will give you rain in due season, and the land shall yield her increase, and the trees of the field shall yield their fruit.

And your threshing shall reach unto the vintage, and the vintage shall reach unto the sowing time: and ye shall eat your bread to the full, and dwell in your land safely. And I will give thee peace in the land, and ye shall lie down, and none shall make you afraid; and I will rid evil beasts out of the land, neither shall the sword go through your land.

And ye shall chase your enemies, and they shall fall before you by the sword. And five of you shall chase an hundred, and an hundred of you shall put ten thousand to flight: and your enemies shall fall before you by the sword. For I will have respect unto you, and make you fruitful, and multiply you, and establish my covenant with you.

And ye shall eat old store, and bring forth the old because of the new. And I will set my tabernacle among you: and my soul shall not abhor you. And I will walk among you, and will be your God, and ye shall be my people.

God we bless your holy name for the whole earth is full of your glory, and we magnify your name in the name of Jesus Christ. Amen.

Prayer to Release the Breaker

Father God in the name of Jesus Christ, we repent for the Kingdom of God has come nigh unto us. God, we thank you for the power of Kingdom of your dear son.

For you said upon mount Zion there shall be deliverance!!!! I will surely assemble, O Jacob, all of thee; I will surely gather the remnant of Israel; I will put them together as the sheep of Bozrah, as the flock in the midst of their fold: they shall make great noise by reason of the multitude of men. The **Breaker** is come up before them: they have broken up, and have passed through the gate, and are gone out by it; and their king shall pass before them and the LORD on the head of them.

For I (the Lord) will go before thee, and make the crooked places straight: I will **break** in pieces the gates of brass, and cut in sunder the bars of iron. God, we thank you for Breaking the gates of Brass and the bars of Iron in the name of Jesus Christ.

For mine Angel shall go before thee, and bring thee in unto the Amorites, and the Hittites, and the Perizzites, and the Canaanites, the Hivites, and the Jebusites: and I will cut them off.

God, send the power of the **Breaker** to destroy every astral, satanic, and voodoo altars; let the power of the **Breaker** hunt down, locate, burn, smash and destroy every altar in the heavens and in the earth that has been used to release spells, curses and devices of every sort, level, order, rank, type, time and place in the name of Jesus Christ according to Duet. 7:5, Hosea 10:2.

For the kings of the earth set themselves, and the rulers take counsel together, against the LORD, and against his anointed, saying, Let us **Break** their bands asunder, and cast away their cords from us. He that sitteth in the heavens shall laugh: the Lord shall have them in derision in the name of Jesus Christ.

Then shall he speak unto them in his wrath, and vex them in his sore displeasure. God, we release your mighty voice to vex and bring sore displeasure against every power and principality that are a spirit help, spirit guide, and a spiritual strengthener to every worker of iniquity that has plotted against our family, business, ministry, Church and lives in the name of Jesus Christ. God, **Break** their ranks of sickness, poverty, and disease with a rod of iron according to Psalm 2:9.

Break thou the arm of the wicked and the evil man; seek out his wickedness till thou find none. The LORD is King forever and ever: the heathen are perished out of his land in the name of Jesus Christ.

Break their teeth, O God, in their mouth; break out the great teeth of the young lions, O LORD. Let them melt away as waters which run continually: when he bendeth his bow to shoot his arrows, let them be as cut in pieces.

He shall judge the poor of the people; he shall save the children of the needy, and shall break in pieces the oppressor in the name of Yeshua Hamashiah.

God send the **Breaker** to break in pieces the yokes of the Assyrians in the name of Jesus Christ according to Isaiah 14:25, Nah. 1:13.

For his eyes are upon the ways of man, and he seeth all his goings. There is no darkness, nor shadow of death, where the workers of iniquity may hide themselves. For he will not lay upon man more than right; that he should enter into judgment with God.

He shall **Break** in pieces mighty men without number, and set others in their stead. Therefore he knoweth their works, and he overturneth them in the night, so that they are destroyed. He striketh them as wicked men in the open sight of others.

Thus saith the LORD of hosts; Behold, I will **Break** the bow of Elam, the chief of their might. And upon Elam will I bring the four winds from the four quarters of heaven, and will scatter them toward all those winds; and there shall be no nation whither the outcasts of Elam shall not come.

For I will cause Elam to be dismayed before their enemies, and before them that seek their life: and I will bring evil upon them, even my fierce anger, saith the LORD; and I will send the sword after them, till I have consumed them.

God, we release the word of this Judgment against every witch, warlock, Satanist, voodoo and hoodoo doctors, sorcerers, Jezebels, Balaams, Absaloms, diviners, and Belials and every secret group, coven, and confederacy that has plotted, planned and infiltrated our lives, business, church, ministry, job, home to alter and disrupted the vision and the will of God for our lives through witchcraft and Charismatic witchcraft in the name of Jesus Christ according to Jer. 49:35-37.

Therefore, thus saith the Lord GOD, Behold, I am against Pharaoh king of Egypt, and will **Break** his arms, the strong, and that which was broken; and I will cause the sword to fall out of his hand.

God, we thank you for breaking the arm of every strong man, principality, power, throne and dominion that has released physical, spiritual, mental, emotional, and financial oppression over our lives in the name of Jesus Christ.

For God, you spoiled all principalities and powers and brought them to an open shame!!!

God, send the Breaker to break the yoke of poverty from off of our lives, finances, blood line, and mindset in the name of Jesus Christ.

God, send the Breaker to break all sickness and disease from off of our lives in the name of Jesus Christ according to Mic. 2:13.

God, send the Breaker to break the yoke of every spirit of lust and perversion from off of our lives in the name of Jesus Christ according to Nah. 1:13.

God, send the Breaker to break the yoke of mind control and psychic manipulation from off of our lives in the name of Jesus Christ.

God, send the Breaker to break and release us from every ungodly covenants and oaths that were made by ourselves or our ancestors going back 70 generations on both sides of the family; oaths made through witchcraft to idols, groves, devils and satan for wealth, power, position and protection in the name of Jesus Christ.

And the LORD of hosts shall stir up a scourge for him according to the slaughter of Midian at the rock of Oreb: and *as* his rod *was* upon the sea, so shall he lift it up after the manner of Egypt.

And it shall come to pass in that day, *that* his burden shall be taken away from off thy shoulder, and his yoke from off thy neck, and the yoke shall be destroyed because of the anointing.

God, we thank you and praise for the anointing and the power of the breaker in the name of Jesus Christ. Amen.

Prayer Releasing the Voice of the Lord

Father God in the name of Jesus Christ, we repent, for the kingdom of God has come nigh unto us. God, we repent for all disobedience for not hearkening to your voice in the name of Jesus Christ.

For you said and all these blessings shall come on thee, and overtake thee, if thou shalt hearken unto the voice of the LORD thy God. God, we seek to obey your commandments so that we can receive your blessing in the name of Jesus Christ according to Duet. 28:1-14.

And the LORD shall cause his glorious voice to be heard, and shall shew the lighting down of his arm, with the indignation of his anger, and with the flame of a devouring fire, with scattering, and tempest, and hailstones, let this be released upon our enemies in the name of Jesus Christ.

For through the voice of the LORD shall the Assyrian be beaten down, which smote with a rod. And in every place where the grounded staff shall pass, which the LORD shall lay upon him, it shall be with tabrets and harps: and in battles of shaking will he fight with it.

Let God arise and all our enemies be scattered. God, let every witch, warlock, sorcerers, enchanters, Jezebels, belials, voodoo, hoodoo practitioners, every worker of iniquity and their attendants that has targeted us, our families, business, ministry, anointing, and the purpose and plan that God has ordained for our lives be scattered in the name of Jesus Christ.

Hear the word of the LORD, ye that tremble at his word. Your brethren that hated you, that cast you out for my name's sake, said, Let the LORD be glorified: but he shall appear to your joy, and they shall be ashamed. A voice of noise from the city, a voice from the temple, a voice of the LORD that rendereth recompense to his enemies.

God let Isaiah 30:30-32, 66:5-6 and the voice of the Almighty locate, hunt down, and manifest in the lives of every worker of iniquity until they have either repented unto true salvation or until they and their confederates, cohorts, underlings, spirit guides, helps, and attendants are utterly destroyed with fire and brimstone in the name of Yeshua Hamashiah.

God let your voice, the voice of the Almighty release the Glory of God from your throne room, upon our lives and situation in the name of Jesus Christ according to Ezek 10:4-6.

We release the voice of the Lord to speak to our star and command it to realign itself to its proper time and place in the name of Jesus Christ.

We release the voice of the Lord to curse every work of iniquity issued against our health, forward progress, and success in the name of Jesus Christ according to Mark 11:14, 20.

We release the voice of the Lord to speak unto every mountain, mountains of poverty, sickness, and disease be thou removed and be thou cast into the sea in the name of Jesus Christ.

Give unto the LORD, O ye mighty, give unto the LORD glory and strength. Give unto the LORD the glory due unto his name; worship the LORD in the beauty of holiness.

The voice of the LORD is upon the waters: the God of glory thundereth: the LORD is upon many waters.

The voice of the LORD is powerful; the voice of the LORD is full of majesty.

The voice of the LORD breaketh the cedars; yea, the LORD breaketh the cedars of Lebanon. He maketh them also to skip like a calf; Lebanon and Sirion like a young unicorn.

The voice of the LORD divideth the flames of fire.

The voice of the LORD shaketh the wilderness; the LORD shaketh the wilderness of Kadesh.

The voice of the LORD maketh the hinds to calve, and discovereth the forests: and in his temple doth every one speak of his glory.

The LORD sitteth upon the flood; yea, the LORD sitteth King forever.

The LORD will give strength unto his people; the LORD will bless his people with peace.

God, we thank you for lifting up your voice against every demonic plot, plan, devises that have been and will be assigned against our lives as a barrier of hindrance, stagnation, delays, abortions, hurt, harm, or danger and we give you the praise in the name of Jesus Christ. Amen.

Prayer to Release the Angels

Father God in the name of Jesus Christ, God, we give you glory and praise, we repent for the kingdom of God has come nigh unto us.

God we thank you for your presence and for your response to this prayer. God, we ask that you send your angels to encamp round about us in the name of Jesus Christ.

And the angel of God, which went before the camp of Israel, removed and went behind them; and the pillar of the cloud went from before their face, and stood behind them.

And it came between the camp of the Egyptians and the camp of Israel; and it was a cloud and darkness to them, but it gave light by night to these: so that the one came not near the other all the night.

God, send the angel of God to be a light unto our paths and to be gross perpetual darkness to our enemies in the name of Jesus Christ.

Behold, I send an Angel before thee, to keep thee in the way, and to bring thee into the place which I have prepared. Beware of him, and obey his voice, provoke him not; for he will not pardon your transgressions: for my name *is* in him.

But if thou shalt indeed obey his voice, and do all that I speak; then I will be an enemy unto thine enemies, and an adversary unto thine adversaries. For mine Angel shall go before thee, and bring thee in unto the Amorites, and the Hittites, and the Perizzites, and the Canaanites, the Hivites, and the Jebusites: and I will cut them off.

God, send your angels to encourage us, as we go in your might into battle in the name of Jesus Christ according to Judges 6:12-14.

They fought from heaven; the stars in their courses fought against Sisera. The river of Kishon swept them away, that ancient river, the river Kishon. O my soul, thou hast trodden down strength. Then were the horse hoofs broken by the means of the pransings, the pransings of their mighty ones.

And it came to pass that night that the angel of the LORD went out, and smote in the camp of the Assyrians an hundred fourscore and five thousand: and when they arose early in the morning.

God let you angels go to battle with us and for us against our strong enemies according to the scriptures that were just read in the name of Jesus Christ.

God send you angels to keep watch, give warnings and to evacuate us out places due for judgment and destruction in the name of Jesus Christ according to Gen. 28: 15, 19:15-20.

God we thank you for your angels being with us in every situation in the name of Yeshua Hamashiah according to Gen. 32: 1-2.

For he shall give his angels charge over thee, to keep thee in all thy ways. They shall bear thee up in their hands, lest thou dash thy foot against a stone.

God send your angels to minister to us after demonic encounters in the name of Jesus Christ according to Matt 4:11.

The Son of man shall send forth his angels, and they shall gather out of his kingdom all things that offend, and them which do iniquity; and shall cast them into a furnace of fire: there shall be wailing and gnashing of teeth.

So shall it be at the end of the world: the angels shall come forth, and sever the wicked from among the just, and shall cast them into the furnace of fire: there shall be wailing and gnashing of teeth.

God send your angels to stop every witch, warlock, sorcerer, hoodoo and voodoo practitioner, satanist, jezebel, and balaam in their path in the name of Jesus Christ according to Num. 22:24, 31.

Seeing it is a righteous thing with God to recompense tribulation to them that trouble you; and to you who are troubled rest with us, when the Lord Jesus shall be revealed from heaven with his mighty angels, In flaming fire taking vengeance on them that know not God, and that obey not the gospel of our Lord Jesus Christ. Who shall be punished with everlasting destruction from the presence of the Lord, and from the glory of his power.

God send your angels to go to war with us against every demonic force of poverty, sickness, backwardness, stagnation, sabotage, misfortune in the name of Jesus Christ according to Judges 5:20.

The chariots of God are twenty thousand, even thousands of angels: the Lord is among them, as in Sinai, in the holy place.

God we thank you for the chariots of God, your mighty angels for moving every demonic force out of their position of power for a rapid change in our lives in the name of Jesus Christ.

God send your angel to speak to us in our dreams in the name of Jesus Christ according to Gen 31:11.

God send your mighty angels to prosper us in thy way in the name of Jesus Christ according to Gen 24:40.

And he saith unto him, Verily, verily, I say unto you, hereafter ye shall see heaven open, and the angels of God ascending and descending upon the Son of man.

God we thank you for opening the heavens over our lives, over our situation in the name of Jesus Christ.

And God, we thank you and praise you for you are the Lord of Lords and the King of Kings.

The LORD hath prepared his throne in the heavens; and his kingdom ruleth over all. Bless the LORD, ye his angels that excel in strength, that do his commandments, hearkening unto the voice of his word.

Bless ye the LORD, all ye his hosts; ye ministers of his, that do his pleasure. Bless the LORD, all his works in all places of his dominion: bless the LORD, O my soul.

Prayer to Release the Blessing of the Kingdom

Father God in the name of Jesus Christ, God, we repent and ask for you to forgive our sins in the name of Jesus Christ. For you said if we confess our sins you are faithful and just to forgive us and the blood of Jesus Christ shall cleanse us from all unrighteousness.

Blessed *is* the man that walketh not in the counsel of the ungodly, nor standeth in the way of sinners, nor sitteth in the seat of the scornful. But his delight *is* in the law of the LORD; and in his law doth he meditate day and night. And he shall be like a tree planted by the rivers of water, that bringeth forth his fruit in his season; his leaf also shall not wither; and whatsoever he doeth shall prosper.

Blessed *be* the Lord, *who* daily loadeth us *with benefits, even* the God of our salvation. We bless you God in the name of Jesus Christ according to Psalm 68:19.

For God you said, And I will bless them that bless thee, and curse him that curseth thee; and in thee shall all families of the earth be blessed. God, we thank you for blessing those that bless us and for cursing those who curse us in the name of Jesus Christ according to Gen. 12:3.

God we release the 10 plagues of Egypt along with every returned curse to the sender; we seal the curses upon the heads of those who would curse us in the name of Jesus Christ.

God we destroy the vocal cords of the wicked that would overthrow our ordained blessings in the name of Jesus Christ; for God, you would not hearken unto Balaam; therefore he blessed you still: so I delivered you out of his hand.

God deliver us out of every hand of Balaam, Jezebel, and every type of worker of iniquity in the name of the Lord Jesus Christ.

God, bless those that have welcomed us in the name of Jesus Christ according to Gen 39:5.

God, we ask that you bless those that are orphaned and that are separated from their love one's in the name of Jesus Christ according to Duet 33:16.

God, we ask that you bless us so that we can be a blessing to others in the name of Jesus Christ according to Duet 33:7.

Blessed are the poor in spirit: for theirs is the kingdom of heaven. Blessed are they that mourn: for they shall be comforted. Blessed are the meek: for they shall inherit the earth. Blessed are they which do hunger and thirst after righteousness: for they shall be filled.

Blessed are the merciful: for they shall obtain mercy. Blessed are the pure in heart: for they shall see God. Blessed are the peacemakers: for they shall be called the children of God. Blessed are they which are persecuted for righteousness' sake: for theirs is the kingdom of heaven.

Blessed are ye, when men shall revile you, and persecute you, and shall say all manner of evil against you falsely, for my sake. Rejoice, and be exceeding glad: for great is your reward in heaven: for so persecuted they the prophets which were before you.

Who shall ascend into the hill of the LORD? or who shall stand in his holy place? He that hath clean hands, and a pure heart; who hath not lifted up his soul unto vanity, nor sworn deceitfully. He shall receive the blessing from the LORD, and righteousness from the God of his salvation.

God let the blessings of the Lord be upon us as a mark from heaven in the name of Jesus Christ according to Psalm 129:4-8.

Christ hath redeemed us from the curse of the law, being made a curse for us. For it is written, cursed is every one that hangeth on a tree; that the blessing of Abraham might come on the Gentiles through Jesus Christ; that we might receive the promise of the Spirit through faith in the name of Jesus Christ according to Gal 3:13-14.

And all these blessings shall come on thee, and overtake thee, if thou shalt hearken unto the voice of the LORD thy God. Blessed shalt thou be in the city, and blessed shalt thou be in the field. Blessed shall be the fruit of thy body, and the fruit of thy ground, and the fruit of thy cattle, the increase of thy kind, and the flocks of thy sheep, blessed shall be thy basket and thy store.

Blessed shalt thou be when thou comest in, and blessed shalt thou be when thou goest out. The LORD shall cause thine enemies that rise up against thee to be smitten before thy face: they shall come out against thee one way, and flee before thee seven ways.

The LORD shall command the blessing upon thee in thy storehouses, and in all that thou settest thine hand unto; and he shall bless thee in the land which the LORD thy God giveth thee according to Deut 28:2-8.

Then Isaac sowed in that land in the time of famine, and received in the same year an hundredfold: and the LORD blessed him. And the man waxed great, and went forward, and grew until he became very great: For he had possession of flocks, and possession of herds, and great store of servants: and the Philistines envied him.

God we speak life to every seed we have sown through tithes, offerings, fastings, prayers, praise, worship, and adoration to bring forth a hundred fold harvests in the name of the Lord Jesus Christ.

God we ask that you bless us with a protective hedge according to Job 1:10;

So the LORD blessed the latter end of Job more than his beginning: God, we ask that you bless our latter days in the name of Jesus Christ according to Job 42:12.

God, we ask that you bless our house, office, business, job, and every temporary dwelling with the fullness of your presence in the name of Jesus Christ, for it was told that the Lord blessed the house of Obededom and all that belongs to him because of the Ark of God.

God, we bow our heads and we bless you in the name of Jesus Christ according to Neh. 8:6.

Blessed *be* the LORD, because he hath heard the voice of my supplications. The LORD *is* my strength and my shield; my heart trusted in him, and I am helped: therefore my heart greatly rejoiceth; and with my song will I praise him.

The LORD *is* their strength, and he *is* the saving strength of his anointed. Save thy people, and bless thine inheritance: feed them also, and lift them up forever. God, we thank you and praise you in the name of Yeshua Hamashiah. Amen.

Releasing the Power of God for Miracle Provision

Father God in the name of Jesus Christ, we repent for the Kingdom of God has come nigh unto thee; we repent from sin and unforgiveness in the name of Jesus Christ. Purge us with hyssop so we can be clean wash us and I will be whiter than snow.

God, in these end times we acknowledge you as our source of provision for housing, food, finances, good health and clothing in the name of Jesus Christ.

And Elisha said unto her, What shall I do for thee? Tell me, what hast thou in the house? And she said, Thine handmaid hath not anything in the house, save a pot of oil. Then he said, Go, borrow thee vessels abroad of all thy neighbors, even empty vessels; borrow not a few. And when thou art come in, thou shalt shut the door upon thee and upon thy sons, and shalt pour out into all those vessels, and thou shalt set aside that which is full. So she went from him, and shut the door upon her and upon her sons, who brought the vessels to her; and she poured out. And it came to pass, when the vessels were full, that she said unto her son, Bring me yet a vessel. And he said unto her, there is not a vessel more. And the oil stayed. Then she came and told the man of God. And he said, Go, sell the oil, and pay thy debt, and live thou and thy children off the rest.

God, we ask that you manifest this scripture according to the emergencies and necessities in our lives in the name of Yeshua Hamashiah according to 2Kings 4:2-7.

God, we ask that you manifest the miracle of manna in our lives, over our finances for your glory in the name of Jesus Christ according to Exodus 16:15-16.

This is the thing which the LORD hath commanded. Gather of it every man according to his eating, an omer for every man, according to the number of your persons; take ye every man for them which are in his tents. And the children of Israel did so, and gathered some more, some less.

God, in these end time we acknowledge you as our source of provision and we thank you for the gathering of manifold blessings and miracle provisions released from your Hand to our hand on a daily basis in the name of Jesus Christ.

Lord Jesus, we thank you for you said I will provide all your needs according to your riches in glory.

God, bless us so that we would be able to give and to share with others in the name of Jesus Christ according to Matt. 17:27.

God, bless us so that we would be able to provide, clothes and feed the needy in the name of Jesus Christ according to Matt. 15:36-39.

God, we thank you for miracle provisions to get our ministry going in the name of Jesus Christ according to Exodus 16:16.

God, we thank you for miracle provisions to keep our ministry going in the name of Jesus Christ 2Kings 4:2-7.

God, we thank you for miracle provisions for paying all of our utility and household bills and expenses in the name of Jesus Christ according to Mark 6:41-43.

The LORD shall command the blessing upon thee in thy storehouses, and in all that thou settest thine hand unto; and he shall bless thee in the land which the LORD thy God giveth thee.

Thine, O LORD, is the greatness, and the power, and the glory, and the victory, and the majesty: for all that is in the heaven and in the earth is thine; thine is the kingdom, O LORD, and thou art exalted as head above all.

Both riches and honor come of thee, and thou reignest over all; and in thine hand is power and might; and in thine hand it is to make great, and to give strength unto all. Now therefore, our God, we thank thee, and praise thy glorious name.

And God, we thank you for our expectation is in you and your miracle working power of provision in the name of Yeshua Hamashiah. Amen.

Prayer for Business Breakthroughs

Father in the name of Jesus Christ, we ask that you destroy with fire every barrier that is design to abort every "at the point of breakthrough" in business according to Jer. 51:58.

God, we ask that you send fire to destroy every barrier that would cause people not to accept or return phone calls in the name of Jesus Christ.

God, we forgive every person, that we have an aught with for whatever reason, that the accuser of the brethren has used to block our blessings, in the name of Jesus Christ.

For you said that if we confess our sins you are faithful and just to forgive us and the blood of Jesus Christ will cleanse us from all unrighteousness.

We destroy every barrier of mental discouragement and misfortune in the name of Jesus Christ.

We destroy with the finger of God every barrier that would cause us to give up on our plans, hopes and dreams in the name of Jesus Christ according to Luke 11:20.

Holy Ghost fire disintegrate ever satanic contract of failure programmed into our star in the name of Jesus Christ.

We command the finger of God to locate and cast out every host of hell that forms barriers of sabotage that has been programmed into my life at the point of breakthrough according to Luke 11:20-22, 2Pet. 2:4.

We destroy with fire every barrier that would cause us to give up on our dreams in the name of Jesus Christ.

We destroy with fire every barrier of failure that has been designed to attach itself to my business plans and my personal breakthroughs in the name of Jesus Christ according Joel 2:3.

But thou shalt remember the LORD thy God: for it is he that giveth thee power to get wealth that he may establish his covenant which he sware unto thy fathers, as it is this day.

We release the sons of Issachar anointing to know the time and the seasons, and also the ingenuity on what to say, and what to do. God, we thank you for reprogramming us to go forward in life in the name of Jesus Christ according to Ezek 1:9.

We command the favor of God to over throw every barrier of failure in our life in the name of Jesus Christ.

God release the favor of God, to attach itself to my business plans, phone calls, faxes, e-mails, and proposals; for thou LORD wilt bless the righteous; with favor wilt thou compass him as *with* a shield. God, let your favor compass the works of our hands in the name of Jesus Christ.

And the LORD was with Joseph, and he was a prosperous man; and he was in the house of his master the Egyptian. And his master saw that the LORD was with him, and that the LORD made all that he did to prosper in his hand.

Lord God, we continue to seek you for you will, God cause us to prosper in the name of Jesus Christ according to 2Chr. 26:5.

Every man also to whom God hath given riches and wealth, and hath given him power to eat thereof, and to take his portion, and to rejoice in his labor; this *is* the gift of God.

And he shall be like a tree planted by the rivers of water, that bringeth forth his fruit in his season; his leaf also shall not wither; and whatsoever he doeth shall prosper.

Lord we give you glory and the honor for your word and we praise you for the manifestation in the name of Jesus Christ.

Keep back thy servant also from presumptuous sins; let them not have dominion over me: then shall I be upright, and I shall be innocent from the great transgression. Let the words of my mouth, and the meditation of my heart, be acceptable in thy sight, O LORD, my strength, and my redeemer.

And it shall be, when the LORD thy God shall have brought thee into the land which he swore unto thy fathers, to Abraham, to Isaac, and to Jacob, to give the great and goodly cities, which thou buildeth not, And houses full of all good *things*, which thou fillest not, and wells dug, which thou diggest not, vineyards and olive trees, which thou plantest not; when thou shalt have eaten and be full.

O thou afflicted, tossed with tempest, and not comforted, behold, I will lay thy stones with fair colors, and lay thy foundations with sapphires. And I will make thy windows of agates, and thy gates of carbuncles, and all thy borders of pleasant stones.

And all thy children shall be taught of the LORD; and great shall be the peace of thy children. In righteousness shalt thou be established: thou shalt be far from oppression; for thou shalt not fear: and from terror; for it shall not come near thee. Behold, they shall surely gather together, but not by me: whosoever shall gather together against thee shall fall for thy sake.

Behold, I have created the smith that bloweth the coals in the fire, and that bringeth forth an instrument for his work; and I have created the waster to destroy. No weapon that is formed against thee shall prosper; and every tongue that shall rise against thee in judgment thou shalt condemn.

Then beware lest thou forget the LORD, which brought thee forth out of the land of Egypt, from the house of bondage. Thou shalt fear the LORD thy God, and serve him, and shalt swear by his name.

Call it Forth
(John 11:43)

Father God in the name of Yeshua Hamashiah, we call forth every promise, every vision, every prophecy from your mouth that has been hindered, delayed and illegally aborted by every satanic force of every sort, level, order, and rank, we call forth the angels that are assigned and responsible for their manifestations to plow through the forces of the enemy in the name of Jesus Christ according Psalm 103:20.

We call forth Michael and his angels to prevail on our behalf according to Rev. 12:7-8, we bind, curse, burn, abort, and destroy all satanic delays and abortions released on our destiny and everything that pertains to every prophecy and every promise, every prayer, and every blessing of wealth and good health in the name of Jesus Christ.

We command the morning, the dayspring, the sun moon and stars to know its place to realign our star in the heavens, and to shake all wickedness from off our destiny in the name of Jesus Christ according to Job 38:12-13.

Father in the name of Jesus Christ we call forth the same spirit that raised Jesus from the dead to resurrect every prophecy, every promise, every vision, every inventive business idea, that is the will of God for our lives.

We call forth, through faith of the operation of God, the resurrection of everything that has been aborted by all witchcraft, envy, jealousy, psychic prayers, Jezebelic prayers chains, well meaning prayers that are not God's will for our lives, spoken word curses, spoken word curses from the womb, and all blood line curses that aid as a doorway for sabotage.

All satanic delays of backwardness, stagnation, still born births, spiritual abortions, and premature births, Lord we repent for our sins and the sins of our fathers according to Lev 26:40-42, and close every door at the point of entry according to Rev 3:7.

God!!!! In the name of Jesus, we call forth your Angels with everlasting chains according Jude 1:6 to bind up and spoil the goods of every strong man according to Mark 3:27.

We shout the sword of the Lord and of Gideon according to Judges 7:20-22 to release confusion and a perverse spirit according to Isaiah 19:14-16, upon every demonic confederacy that's assembled and those that are trying to regroup, reorganize, and reassemble themselves in the natural and the supernatural.

We call forth destruction and annihilation according to Jer 50:25-26. For the Lord shall go forth as a mighty man, he shall stir up jealousy like a man of war: he shall cry, yea, roar; he shall prevail against his enemies.

So Lord, we thank you and praise you and give you the glory for the release and accelerated manifestation of every covenant promise of wealth and good health to fulfill our destiny for the glory of the kingdom of God in the name of Jesus Christ. Amen.

Releasing the Release

Father God in the name of Jesus Christ we repent for any sins of omission and sins of commission that are helping the enemy to stop, block and abort our release of covenant blessing of wealth and good health in the name of Jesus Christ.

God we ask that you open up your armory, and release your angels and the weapons of war according to Jer 50:25, to break forth and release every person, ministry, and business entity that are called and ordained to bless us for the glory of the Kingdom of God in the name of the Lord Jesus Christ.

We rebuke the enemy and we bind their kings with chains and there nobles with fetters of iron that has bound the mind's and the hearts of those ordained to bless us in the name of Yeshua Hamashiah according to Psalm 149:8-10, Isaiah 6:5-8.

God we release the whirlwind of the Lord to go forth with fury against every opposing prayer, chant, curse, and prophetic satanic utterances that have been summoned and assigned to delay, sabotage, and abort the release of every promise, blessing, prophecy, and prayer that's the will of God for our lives in the name of Jesus Christ according to Jer 30:16-17, 22-24. We speak life, and call those things that are not as thou they were according Rom. 4:17.

Let the fierce anger of the Lord not return until HE have done it, until he have performed the intents of HIS heart according to Psalm 103:20.

Blessed shalt thou be when thou comest in, and blessed shalt thou be when thou goest out. The LORD shall cause thine enemies that rise up against thee to be smitten before thy face: they shall come out against thee one way, and flee before thee seven ways.

The LORD shall command the blessing upon thee in thy storehouses, and in all that thou settest thine hand unto; and he shall bless thee in the land which the LORD thy God giveth thee.

The LORD shall establish thee an holy people unto himself, as he hath sworn unto thee, if thou shalt keep the commandments of the LORD thy God, and walk in his ways. And all people of the earth shall see that thou art called by the name of the LORD; and they shall be afraid of thee. And the LORD shall make thee plenteous in goods, in the fruit of thy body, and in the fruit of thy cattle, and in the fruit of thy ground, in the land which the LORD sware unto thy fathers to give thee.

The LORD shall open unto thee his good treasure, the heaven to give the rain unto thy land in his season, and to bless all the work of thine hand: and thou shalt lend unto many nations, and thou shalt not borrow.

And God, we thank you for the Releasing the release and the restoration of favor, wealth and good health, and every covenant Blessings that you have ordained for our life in these end times in the name of Jesus Christ.

As the dew of Hermon, and as the dew that descended upon the mountains of Zion: for there the LORD commanded the blessing, even life for evermore.

Now God, we praise you and we bless your Holy name for the whole earth is full of your Glory and we give you the praise in the name of Yeshua Hamashiah. Amen!!!

Releasing the Grace of God

Father in the name of Jesus Christ, we repent for the kingdom of God has come nigh unto us.

O LORD God of hosts, hear my prayer: give ear, O God of Jacob. Selah. Behold, O God our shield, and look upon the face of thine anointed. For a day in thy courts is better than a thousand. I had rather be a doorkeeper in the house of my God, than to dwell in the tents of wickedness.

For the LORD God is a sun and shield: the LORD will give grace and glory: no good thing will he withhold from them that walk uprightly.

God, we ask that you pour your Grace upon our lips in the name of Jesus Christ according to Psalm 45:2.

God, we ask that you release your grace and glory upon our lives in the name of Jesus Christ according to Prov 3:34, Luke 2:40.

Jesus we thank you for your grace in the forgivingness and the forsaking of our sins in the name of Jesus Christ.

God dwell among us in grace in the name of Jesus Christ according to John 1:14, 16.

God let your grace be bestowed upon us in the name of Jesus Christ according to Acts 11:23.

God let your grace be upon on us for ministry in the name of Jesus Christ. And with great power gave the apostles witness of the resurrection of the Lord Jesus; and great grace was upon them all. Neither was there any among them that lacked.

God let us walk in your Grace for signs and wonders to be wrought by our hands in the name of Jesus Christ according to Acts 14:3.

And now, brethren, I commend you to God, and to the word of his grace, which is able to build you up, and to give you an inheritance among all them which are sanctified.

God we ask that you connect our faith to the abundance of your grace in the name of Jesus Christ according to Acts 5:15.

God we ask for a revelation of your grace to walk in the fullness of your redemption in the name of Jesus Christ according to Rom 5:15.

God we thank for the grace of God locating and releasing itself on your end time remnant in the name of Jesus Christ according to Rom. 11:5.

God we thank you for the full power of your grace in our lives to crush the power of satan in the name of Jesus Christ according to Rom. 16:20.

For all things *are* for your sakes, that the abundant grace might through the thanksgiving of many redound to the glory of God. For which cause we faint not; but though our outward man perish, yet the inward *man* is renewed day by day. For our light affliction, which is but for a moment, worketh for us a far more exceeding *and* eternal weight of glory.

For ye know the grace of our Lord Jesus Christ, that, though he was rich, yet for your sakes he became poor, that ye through his poverty might be rich.

God give us the focus to grow in your grace in the name of Jesus Christ according to 2 Pet 3:18.

God give us to know the manifold grace of God in the name of Jesus Christ according to 1 Pet 4:10.

God let us find grace in our time of need in the name of Yeshua Hamashiah according to Heb 4:16.

Father let the grace of the Lord Jesus be with our spirit in the name of Yeshua Hamashiah according to Gal.6:18.

Let the word of Christ dwell in you richly in all wisdom; teaching and admonishing one another in psalms and hymns and spiritual songs, singing with grace in your hearts to the Lord.

May the grace of our Lord Jesus Christ be with you all, Amen.

To order a Copy of Blitzkrieg: The Art of War in the Spirit
Go to amazon.com or createspace.com/3374692
Price is $13.00

To order a copy of Getting into Position: The Remnant of Jacob
Go to amazon.com or to Createspace.com/3389564
Price is $10.00

Discounts will be available for all bulk orders and book store distributers.

Other titles will be available very shortly.

To contact me for meetings, seminars, revivals, mass deliverances please email me at. And I will get back in contact with You

Thank you and my God bless you.

  Shalom

tonygeorgeministries@gmail.com

myspace.com/tonygeorgeministries

facebook.com/remnantofjacob

Made in the USA
Columbia, SC
17 March 2023

13944884R00107